CHINESE
NAMES

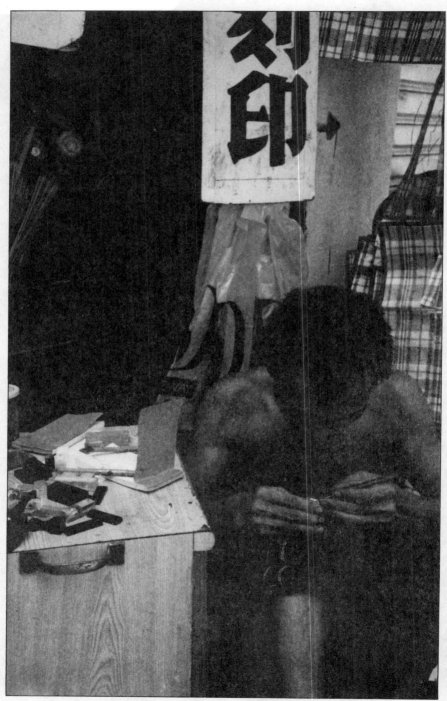

A street vendor sculpting a name seal in Fuzhou, China.

CHINESE NAMES

THE TRADITIONS SURROUNDING
THE USE OF CHINESE SURNAMES
AND PERSONAL NAMES

RUSSELL JONES

Pelanduk
Publications

Published by
Pelanduk Publications (M) Sdn. Bhd.
(Co. No. 113307-W)
24 Jalan 20/16A, 46300 Petaling Jaya,
Selangor Darul Ehsan,
Malaysia.

All correspondence to:
Pelanduk Publications (M) Sdn. Bhd.,
P.O. Box 8265, 46785 Kelana Jaya,
Selangor Darul Ehsan, Malaysia.

Perpustakaan Negara Malaysia   Cataloguing-in-Publication Data

Jones, Russell, 1926-
    Chinese names: the traditions surrounding the use of Chinese
    surnames and personal names / Russell Jones
    ISBN 967-978-619-6
    1. Names, Personal — Chinese. I. Title
    929.40951

Printed by
Potensi Serentak Sdn. Bhd.

Contents

Illustrations

Introduction

"We may then confidently assert that name-giving has always been considered in China a matter of high importance"[*]

A word of explanation is needed for this compilation of data concerning the names used by the Chinese in Malaysia, to define its scope, and its limitations. In the 1950s I found myself working in the Immigration Department headquarters in Pulau Pinang. It was part of our task to record the names of the Chinese who constituted the majority of our customers; the more I delved into this the more fascinated I became. With the generous cooperation of Chinese colleagues, three aids to our work were compiled. The first was a register of all the Chinese words which turned up as surnames or personal names, arranged according to their number in the Chinese Commercial Code, giving for each the spellings that we came across in the various dialects, the 'district name' (see Appendix F) and other data. The second was an alphabetical index of the spellings in Mandarin as well as the dialects, to enable us to find the names in our register. The third was an account of the customs associated with the ways the names were used. This latter was published in 1959 by the Malayan Branch of the Royal Asiatic Society under the title "Chinese Names".

It was reprinted subsequently by Pelanduk Publications, and in 1994 I undertook to enlarge it and bring it more up-to-date. For this I have used materials gathered since 1960, and in 1995 was fortunate enough to spend two weeks in Pulau Pinang tying up loose ends.

It will become evident that this study is not rigorously confined to the Chinese in Malaysia at the present time: where it would throw light on what I was discussing, I have not hesitated to utilize data on traditional practices in China, sometimes from long ago. Drawing widely upon 19th century writers, in places I invoke what is virtually a legendary culture that exists no longer in China, (and perhaps never did exist except in the belief of the

---

[*] J.J.M. de Groot, 1910, Volume VI:1138.

folk, or perhaps only in the eyes of foreign observers). In this way I have tried to build up a coherent framework in which present-day practices can be understood in the light of past beliefs.

This somewhat eclectic approach may leave the reader with no means of knowing whether a particular piece of information was obtained from an informant in the 1950s, (when I carried out most of my inquiries,) or earlier or later than that.

This does not trouble me greatly, I have simply tried to give an account which reflects the interest of the topic, with its variety and its continuity, and which will offer lines of thought to any one who is attracted towards any aspect of it; for those inclined to pursue particular aspects, I have offered numerous bibliographical references.

Appendix A, incorporating a compilation of surnames ("The Hundred Names"), is of particular interest. A striking indication of the significance of names in Chinese thinking can be gleaned from the fact that this was one of the three primary texts taught to Chinese children in the past. This compilation is still widely used, and reprinted annually in the almanacs. Appendix H emphasizes the quintessentially traditional character of the almanacs in which the lists of names are published. This gives us ample justification for making a study of Chinese names as an ancient tradition, not simply as a current social phenomenon.

But this is not to deny the need, and scope, for fieldwork to establish the present-day position in Malaysia and elsewhere in South East Asia. For example: How many of the surnames in the published lists are in actual use here? To what extent are the old traditional links between surnames and specific "district names" valid for Malaysia? In other words our study of the tradition need not preclude research to establish how far that tradition is applicable at the present time. The two aspects should be complementary.

Where appropriate, referring to the past, I have used "Malaya" in its traditional sense, to denote the Malay Peninsula and Singapore. Otherwise I have used "Malaysia", but in this context what is true of Malaysia is generally true of Singapore too.

I have given many examples by way of illustrating the material; it is hoped that these will compensate for some of the shortcomings of the descriptions of customs associated with naming.

Orthography

Choice of spellings can be a problem with such a subject. Pure Sinologists might like to find all the names in the Mandarin pronunciation. But for people accustomed to seeing the names in the pronunciations of the different dialects and in the spellings commonly used (however inconsistent) this is confusing. Mrs Goh is not immediately recognizable as Mrs "Wu", or Mr Huat as Mr "Fa". Where I have given the Mandarin forms of technical terms, or in lists of names, I have endeavoured to give also the Hokkien form, that being the majority dialect. Where I have marked it "Amoy" rather than "Hokkien", it is in the system of romanization used in the Dictionary of Carstairs Douglas. Owing to the limitations of the font, the tone marks have often been omitted. For other cases, the spelling of the names as they were found has been preserved.

For the Mandarin pronunciation the Wade-Giles system of spelling is still preferred by many writers, and I use that freely. Pinyin spelling is coming into increasing use, and that has been used as well, especially in the lists of surnames. To ease the path of the embryonic Sinologist I have freely interspersed Chinese commercial code numbers and references to the dictionaries of Mathews and Giles (for publication details see 'Sources').

My acknowledgements to those who assisted me are given on p.viii.

To conclude: As Tan Pow Tek (1924:3) observed, after reflecting on the difficulties of his task "any compiler of Chinese surnames has to breathe a long breath, wrinkle his face, nod his head and dig out his brains deeper, or else he should give up the job as hopeless or curiously impossible a task". He knew!

R J

Some abbreviations

Cant.	Cantonese
Hok.	Hokkien (Fujian, Minnanhua)
Md.	Mandarin (Putonghua)
Py.	Pinyin ("Phonetic spelling")
'C' or 'CCC'	Chinese Commercial Code number
'M'	Mathews' Chinese-English Dictionary
'G'	Giles' Chinese-English Dictionary.

Acknowledgements

I gratefully acknowledge the assistance of many people during the preparation of these notes, and in connection with my investigations in the 1950s would particularly mention my late and revered Chinese teacher, Ang Tee Hwee of Penang; C.S. Wong of the Chinese Affairs Department, Penang; W.L. Blythe, MCS, CMG; Dr. W.H. Newell; and especially Tham Kok Thye and other colleagues in the Immigration Department.

For more recent help I thank Ms Khoo Su Nin in Penang, and Dr Jan Knappert and Ms Lillian Chia in London. Dr Geoffrey Wade of the University of Hong Kong has been most generous with his help and advice. I am grateful to the Nuffield Foundation for supporting a research visit to Pulau Pinang in 1995. And for this (and all the research I am able to do) I am glad to acknowledge my debt to the incomparable resources of the Library of the School of Oriental and African Studies, University of London.

I The Three Components of the Name

Chinese names generally consist of three words, the first being the surname[1], the latter two being personal names.

The Surname (sometimes called Family Name or Clan Name)
The surname is known in Chinese as 姓 'hsing' (M2770; *Pinyin* xing *Hok.* si[n]) . Giles' definition of 'hsing' is: Originally the clan name of a noble; a surname, defined by the 説文 *Shuo wen* as 人所生也 — that with which a man is born.

The form in Malay and English is 'seh', from Hok. (*Chiang-chew*) 'sè[n]'.

Kiang Kang-Hu in his book *On Chinese Studies* [2] relates that the obligation that all Chinese should have surnames dates from the time of the Emperor Fu Hsi (伏羲 2852BC) — still in what is known as the legendary period of Chinese history. He enumerates (pp.127-8) eighteen sources from which surnames have been derived,

Examples

1. Adopting a dynasty designation	T'ang 唐 Yu 虞 Hsia 夏
2. Taking the name of a feudal territory or division[3]	Chiang 江 Huang 黃 Ch'in 秦 Chin 晉

---

[1] "We put our surname first. This is the natural thing to do, for a man's family always comes before himself" (Rattenbury. 1946:11) .

[2] It will be found on pp.126-8; Dr Newell kindly drew my attention to this book. See Newell, 1962, pp.209-10.

[3] Hauer (1926:120) would include here names which are not at first sight placenames, the radical 邑 [R163, M3037] "a District city" having been dropped from the character. He cites the surname 朱 Chu (Hokkien also Chu) (C2612,

1

3.	Using the name of a political district	Hung 紅 P'an 番 Shen 郴
4.	From the name of a town	Yin 尹 Su 蘇 Mao 毛 Shan 單
5.	From rural hamlets	P'ai 裴 Lu 陸 P'ang 龐 Yen 閻
6.	From cross-roads and stations	Mi 糜 Ts'ai 采 Ou-yang 歐陽
7.	From suburbs of direction, east, west, etc.	Tung-shiang 東鄉 Hsi-men 西門 Nan-yieh 南野
8.	Adopting the personal name of some historical personage	Fu 伏 Yu 禹 T'ang 湯 Chin 金
9.	The use of a man's social name (字) for a family name	K'ung 孔 Fang 方 Kung 貢 T'ung 童
10.	A custom (called Ts'u 次) of adopting the appellation applied to a relative, as old brother, young sister, etc.	Meng 孟 i.e. first brother Chi 季 i.e. last brother Tsu 祖 i.e. grandfather Mi 禰 i.e. grandfather-in-law
11.	From names of tribes or clans	Ching 景 Tso 左 So 素 Chang 掌
12.	From names of official posts[4]	Shih 史 a historian; Chi 籍 a librarian; K'ou 寇 a policeman; Shuai 師 a general; Ssu-T'u 司徒 a civil official. *We may add*

M1346) meaning "red", which he postulates was originally 邦 (Chu, M1353,) the name of a feudal state. Weig (1931:vii) makes the same point. Many names still retain the radical ß, as can be seen from the list of surnames, numbers 6717-6786.

[4] Granet (1930:407) records the nostalgic yearnings of the Chinese for the old days when "those who filled an office kept it till their sons or grandsons were adults; those who exercised a public function took from it their family name and their surname".

2

		Ssu-Ma 司馬 "Keeper of the horses, Minister for war", "General".[5]
13.	From titles of nobility	Huang 皇 emperor Wang 王 king Pa 霸 grand duke Hou 候 duke
14.	From occupations or trades	Wu 巫 a magician T'u 屠 a butcher T'ao 陶 a potter Chiang 匠 a builder
15.	From the name of an object	Chu 車 a carriage Kuan 冠 a hat P'u 蒲 grass Fu 符 a flower
16.	Posthumous titles of rulers	Wen 文 the Literary Wu 武 the Military Chuang 莊 the Polite One Min 閔 the Kindly One
17.	Adding a diminutive to the parent name	Wang-tsu 王子 a King's son Kung-sun 公孫 grandson of a duke; Yuan-po 原伯 the first son of Yuan; Shen-shu 申叔 the third son of Shen
18.	Name of contempt applied to an evil-doer by a ruler (in Chinese it is called an E 惡 name)	Fu 蝮 poisonous snake Mang 莽 rebel Ching 黥 branded felon Hsiao 梟 an owl (a bird of ill omen)

The way the clan names came into being is discussed in some detail by Wojtasiewicz.[6] He postulates other origins for clan names,

---

[5] Creamer (1995:910); Granet (1930:407); see M5585.

for example some come from nicknames (e.g. "the baldheads"); and others from flattering sobriquets (e.g. "the strong").

A number of compilations listing the surnames in current use have been made at different stages of Chinese history. One such, the *Hsu Wen Hsien T'ung K'ao* 續文獻通考 recorded the existence of 4,657 surnames. Other lists have contained varying numbers, 9177[7], 5,730, 4,386, 4,000, etc.[8] Perhaps more realistically, in 1892 Giles[9] published a list containing 1,835 single-character surnames, 216 two-character surnames, and 17 three-character surnames.

But there seems to be a tendency for the number of surnames in common use to be reduced with the passage of time, and I doubt whether this number of surnames would survive in present-day China. In this connection we find that cheap lists of surnames are available in the shops entitled 百家姓 *Po chia hsing* ("The hundred family surnames").[10] There is a Chinese term 百姓 *Po hsing* literally 'One hundred surnames' or 老百姓 *Lao Po Hsing*, 'Old hundred surnames'; this is an idiomatic expression meaning "The People", and should not be taken to mean that there are exactly a hundred surnames in existence.[11] In fact these lists comprise usually between four and five hundred surnames. The list compiled by Tan Pow Tek (see Sources) contains 513 surnames. Giles describes the *Po chia hsing* as "a collection of 438 of the surnames in common use (408 single and 30 double), published at the beginning of the Sung dynasty".[12] The study by Hauer (1926) similarly lists 408 single and 30 double surnames.

---

[6] 1954, e.g. p.39.

[7] Figure given by Lin Shan, 1994:16.

[8] See for example Bauer, 1959:31; Creamer,1995:910.

[9] In the tables appended to his Chinese-English Dictionary, pp.1356-61.

[10] For the origin of the list, and further references, see Hauer, 1926:115-7; and Weig, 1931:v. Both writers make the point that the *Po chia hsing* book was one of the three essential works studied by Chinese schoolchildren; the other two were the *San Tzu Ching* ("Three-character classic") and the *Ch'ien Tzu Wen* ("Thousand-Character Essay").

[11] See discussion by Hauer, 1926:115.

[12] See Giles no.4599 *The Family Surnames*; see Hauer, 1927:75.

But the number varies; one of the lists that I have, published in the 1950s, lists 408 single and 78 two-character surnames; its composition and format are very reminiscent of the Chinese almanacs, from which it may have been taken. Weig's study (1931) also lists 408 single and 78 two-character surnames (see Appendix A).

Of more immediate interest to us is the fact that such a list comprising less than five hundred surnames is found to contain all those ordinarily met with in Malaysia. Our Appendix B lists 479 single-character surnames and 40 two-character surnames. The aim in compiling this list was to include all the surnames that one is likely to encounter in Malaysia. There has been no systematic research to ascertain how many of them are in fact in use in Malaysia. One piece of research in this field is that of Maurice Freedman. At one time he identified 48 surnames in Singapore, and estimated that the total number of surnames in use would be about one hundred; subsequently he revised his estimate to "a little over two hundred"[13] But that is only a rough estimate.

As for the frequency of the more popular names, analysing the surnames of senior civil servants in China a century ago, Giles found that seventy per cent of them shared fifty five surnames.[14] It has been reported more recently that the hundred most common surnames cover no less than eighty-seven per cent of the Chinese in China.[15] Lin Shan also gives 1977 data on the frequency of the surnames in China.[16] The only analysis I have seen of the frequency of surnames in Malaya is that by William Newell. Confining himself to a study of 341 Teochews resident in Malaya, he constructed a table showing the relative fequency of the bearers of fifty Chinese surnames.[17]

---

[13] Freedman, 1957:69; Freedman & Topley, 1961. 'Religion and Social Realignment among the Chinese in Singapore'. *Journal of Asian Studies* 21:6

[14] Giles, p.1355; also in Hauer, 1927:82.

[15] Creamer, 1995:910.

[16] 1994:16-17.

[17] W. H. Newell, 1962:71-72.

To a European, a surname is used as a means of identification, and generally signifies little more than that; but to a Chinese it also connotes a bond with others of the same surname who are still living, and with ancestors who have passed on. Many Chinese believe that all persons bearing the same surname have descended from a common ancestor, that is that they all belong to one lineage; when speaking Chinese, misunderstandings may arise over the interpretation of the terms which in English are 'relative' and 'persons having the same surname', but between which a Chinese does not always bother to distinguish.[18] A Chinese feels a degree of affinity towards other persons who share his surname, although this may not of course be as strong as the bond between actual relatives; this feeling of affinity may be sufficient to find a man employment with an employer who has the same surname,[19] or it may serve as a link to enable him to settle in a particular village where his 'clansmen' have already settled.[20] T'ien Ju-k'ang describes graphically how, when he was carrying out fieldwork in Sarawak in 1949, he was accepted by the residents who shared his surname (田). He writes "I could always find hospitality with other T'iens anywhere in the Colony, and in each district I would be told of T'iens whom I would meet at my next stopping place." As he points out, those T'iens were from separate groups, from Chao An (southern Fukien) and from Hweilai (Kwangtung) respectively, while he himself hailed from Kunming, so that there was no territorial affinity with him, only

---

[18] The usual term in Hokkien is 'chhin lâng' (Pinyin 'qinren'). On the way this term is used, see Freedman, 1957:70-72. But the concept is modified by another, more explicit, Chinese expression: 'T'ung hsing pu t'ung tsung' meaning "Of the same surname but not of the same ancestry" (Giles 4599).

[19] De Groot makes the point that having only employees with the same surname leads to greater trustworthiness in the concern (De Groot, 1885:109-10).

[20] "We should not imagine that they would have emigrated in such large numbers to those distant unknown lands if they had not been convinced beforehand that they would be received with open arms and helped along by former fellow-villagers. They are very well aware that anyone bearing the family name of settlers already established there — thus showing that they had common ancestors, although perhaps from centuries ago — would be certain of getting a livelihood". (De Groot, 1885:113.)

the surname link. It seems furthermore that the two groups mentioned were the closer for being in the Nanyang: "their sense of mutual solidarity may be said to be considerably greater than that existing between two separate local clans of the same surname group in China".[21] Tan Chee-beng records a similar expression of affinity by the Baba whom he was studying, specifically those who shared his surname, 'Tan'. "This created some feeling of amity even though we are not really related".[22]

Clan Associations

We should note one rather remarkable fact about social life in South China. De Groot wrote more than a century ago: " . . if one looks at a Chinese village at all carefully, what immediately attracts the attention is that nearly all the inhabitants bear one and the same family name;" and "most villages of Fuhkien province, ... as a rule are inhabited by people of one clan name only."[23] See Chinben makes a similar comment: "most villages in southeastern China are composed of people with the same surnames."[24] Newell also speaks of "South China where, broadly speaking, village members have one name"[25]. T'ien Ju-k'ang writes specifically of the village of T'ien Chu in Fukien, home of the T'ien clan "No other surnames can be found there."[26] A more recent piece of research into a Hakka community in Hong Kong New Territories also mentions five single-surname Li villages and one

---

[21] T'ien Ju-k'ang, 1956:22,25. One senses that anthropologists' fieldwork is enhanced by such clan connections.

[22] Tan Chee-beng, 1988A:200.

[23] De Groot, 1885:82; De Groot, 1892, Vol.1:191.

[24] Chinben See: Chinese Clanship in the Philippine Setting (JSEAS, 12 no.1, 1981, pp.224,231)

[25] Newell, 1962:209. He qualifies this "If one excludes those people who run shops in the village, who are usually non-relatives for reasons to do with credit, I should estimate that about 70 per cent of Teochiu villages consisted of not more than two surnames" (op.cit., p.17).

[26] T'ien Ju-k'ang, 1956:23.

Wong.[27] We should note that the married women are not included in this generalization, (for reasons which we shall see later,) and there may be a few sons-in-law with different surnames, who have chosen to move in with their wives' families.

At all events this remarkable practice is unknown in the Nanyang. But it does help explain the strength of the clan associations of members bearing the same surname which have been a prominent feature of life here for a century or more. They have played a very important role, especially in view of the fact that to a considerable extent "the surname group as a whole in Sarawak takes the place of the local clan in China."[28] This must hold not only for Sarawak, but the rest of the Nanyang, too.

The clan association is properly known in Chinese as 宗祠 (*Mand.* Tsung Tz'u), but is commonly referred to by local Hokkien Chinese as 'Kong si'[29]. [Giles's dictionary defines this latter term, under entry No.6568, as "公司: a company. Formerly, *the* Company, — the East India Company"]. It is a term now in common use, both in written and spoken Chinese, as well as Indonesian, to refer to commercial companies. Let us see a Malayan Chinese view of the clan association:

> "The early Chinese emigrants came to Malaya principally from Kwangtung or Fukien Province, and those who came from the same village, bearing the same surname, established what are now known as the clan associations or kongsis.
>
> There are two distinct types of clan associations: (1) the family association, or ancestral temple, whose members bear the same surname and (2) the district association, whose members come from the same prefecture or district, but are not necessarily of the same surname.[30]
>
> We are concerned here with the family association only. There is a strong feeling of fraternity amongst the members of

---

[27] Berkowitz et al. 1969:11,14; a further instance is reported by Watson (1986:620).

[28] T'ien Ju-k'ang, 1956:28.

[29] In English 'kongsi' may be used as the equivalent of Chinese lineage (Franke & Chen, 1985, Vol.2 765); but 'kongsi' itself is used in Chinese (Franke & Chen, op.cit., 875).

[30] See Appendix F (District names).

the family association as they are believed to be the direct descendants from the same ancestor or progenitor.

The primary aims of the association were very laudable. The association extended help to newcomers (*Sin-Khek*), giving them accommodation in the premises and finding jobs for them. Scholarship funds were provided for the encouragement of education and mutual-aid schemes for decrepits, old-age and so on were promoted. Ancestral tablets were set up in a sanctuary at the association to perpetuate the memory of the dead.

Today many associations have discarded the original functions intended or laid down by the founders; ..."[31]

One of the functions still maintained by the associations is that of honouring members who have distinguished themselves in academic or public life; the names of these are inscribed on gilded wooden plaques fixed on the wall of the main room in the clan association building. Although as Khoo Keat Siew observes "The constraints of wall space have seen the reduction in size of the plaques and today they have given way to names being inserted on an aluminium board affixed to one of the walls". He makes the point that only men are thus honoured, not women.[32] He was writing of the Khoo Kongsi in Penang, but similar practices can be observed in other clan associations.

A list of common surnames will be found in Appendixes A and B. Before leaving this subject we should note that with certain exceptions (some are mentioned on p.73-76 below), the surname of a father is inherited by his sons and his daughters).

Two-character Surnames
Chinese surnames consisting of more than one character are known in Chinese as 複姓 (*Mand*. Fu-hsing, *Hok*. Hok-seng), or

---

[31] Wu Liu, writing in the Penang *Sunday Gazette* of 8 October 1950. On the clan system in China, see Kiang Kang-hu, 1934 pp.150ff; and for Singapore, see Gamba, Charles, 1966. Chinese Associations in Singapore. JMBRAS 39 pt.2, pp.123-68. For a table of the early Chinese clan associations in Malaya, from 1819 to 1911, see Yen Ching-hwang (1981:88ff).

[32] Khoo Keat Siew, in *Pulau Pinang* Vol.2 No.1 1990:13,14.

雙姓 (*Mand.* Shuang-hsing, *Hok.* Siang-seng).[33] Of the surnames consisting of two characters, as many as seventy-eight may be found in the traditional lists of surnames. Kiang Kang-hu[34] notes that some of them resulted from the transcription of the names of non-Chinese; he adds that "In recent years the custom of having a multi-character name has been very largely discontinued"; and Giles had written much earlier "Of 'double surnames', only two or three are in common use";[35] in Malaysia at all events two-character surnames are extremely rare,[36] with the exception of the three following:

Chinese	In Mandarin	In Hokkien
歐陽	Ou-Yang	Au-Iong[37]
司徒	Ssu-T'u	Su-To[38]
司馬	Ssu-Ma	Su-Ma[39]

The double surnames are used in just the same way as single-character surnames, being followed in the usual way by either one or two personal names. These four examples, being the names of Cantonese women, illustrate the practice:

歐陽亞森   Au Yeong Ah Sim   (The second character is

---

[33] See Weig, 1931:101-124. He lists 78 two-character surnames, giving the Mandarin pronunciation, meaning, etc., of each.

[34] 1934, p.129. The point is also made by Hauer, 1926:120.

[35] Giles, p.1355.

[36] Tan Pow Tek writes (1924:63). "Most of the double surnames are not or rarely found among the Chinese in the British Malaya".

[37] Mentioned in the list on p.2 above. Tan Pow Tek (1924:66) writes that Au-Iong is popular, especially among Hokkiens. Dyer Ball (1900:397) says it is "one of the most common of these bisyllabic surnames in the South of China". Information on it may be found in Weig, 1931:102 and in Hauer, 1927:29-30.

[38] Tan Pow Tek (1924:67) writes that Szi-Tho is popular among the Cantonese. Ssu-T'u is mentioned on p.2 above; more information on it may be found in Weig, 1931:111, and a description of the duties attached to the post can be found in Hauer, 1927:45.

[39] Ssu-Ma is mentioned on p.3 above; information on it may be found in Weig, 1931:101 and in Hauer, 1927:44.

歐陽燕	Au Yang Yin	the same in each case, even though the romanization in the first
歐陽鳳儀	Au Yang Foon Yee	case is Yeong and in the other two cases Yang)
司徒妹	See Thoe Moy	

The lists in Appendixes A and B include the double surnames.

Three-character Surnames

The Rev. W. Campbell's dictionary of the Amoy vernacular includes in an appendix a list of about two thousand surnames; fifteen of these consist each of three characters, for example:

Chinese	In Mandarin	In Hokkien
步鹿根	Pu-Lu-Ken	Po-Lok-Kun
執失代	Chih-Shih-Tai	Chip-Sit-Tai

Possibly these too are transcriptions of foreign surnames; Giles writes "'triple surnames' are practically never met with at all"[40]; in any case, I have never heard of a Chinese in Malaysia having a three-character surname, and for practical purposes their existence can be ignored.

Creamer goes further than this, mentioning a Chinese list which includes nine four-character surnames and three five-character names.[41] Needless to say, these can also be ignored for practical purposes.

Personal Names

In addition to the surname, Chinese have personal names corresponding to the Christian names or given names of the West. As a rule personal names comprise two elements, though single personal names are not uncommon. The personal names as distinct from the surname are generally known as the 名 Ming.

There is not a separate set of words for first and second personal names — in principle words can appear in either

---

[40] 1892, p.1355.

[41] See Creamer, 1995:910.

position — but the first or second slots respectively provide separate functions which can be differentiated in some respects.

The First Given Name (usually the middle name)
The first of the personal names (or the first 'given name') follows the surname and may become the basis for a kind of classificatory description, as opposed to the decidedly individual connotation which, as we shall see, adheres to the second given name.

Generation names

One of the most striking of the classificatory functions is that used to denote the generation of an individual in a particular clan. The custom was to give to brothers and cousins — all those belonging to the same generation — identical elements in their names; in this way the generation they belonged to was made clear. 'Generation names' are known in Chinese by one of these terms

Chinese	In Mandarin	In Amoy Hokkien
字勻	Tzu yün[42]	Jï ûn
派名	P'ai ming[43]	Phài mia^n

But a more general term for 'generation name', favoured by Bauer,[44] is:

排行	P'ai hang	Pâi hâng

According to the dictionaries, this term 'p'ai^2 hang^2' has two meanings. Firstly it denotes (M2754(c)) "the sequence of sons in a family", or (G4624) "the order of sons in a family". In Amoy Hokkien it has the same meaning: "in order of seniority (of brothers)".[45] We shall revert to this meaning later[46].

---

[42] See Bauer, 1957:598.

[43] Mandarin 'p'ai^4' (M4873, G8583) means "to send"; "a clan"; a generation name.

[44] Bauer, 1957:596-8.

[45] See Francken & De Grijs, 1882, p.416.

[46] See p.18.

To give it the unambiguous meaning of 'generation name' we can add a further character making[47]:

排行字　　　P'ai[2] hang[2] tzu[4] [48]　　　Pâi hâng jï

The "generation" P'ai-hang was destined to play a very important role in name-giving. Its first application was in the introductions to genealogies. In Chinese a variety of terms was used for it.

One such term mentioned by Bauer (1957:597) is 輩行 pei[4] hang[2] or pòe hâng (meaning "generation order").[49] Other terms used for 'generation name' are[50] 世派 Shih-p'ai, 派行 P'ai-hang, 字派 Tzu-p'ai, 字倫 Tzu-lun, and 聯名 Lien-ming.

We see then that the generation p'ai-hang by the use of a shared element in the name distinguishes one generation from another. Conventionally it is found as one of the two characters representing the personal name of an individual. This is called a 'full p'ai-hang'. From this we might assume that someone having a personal name consisting of only one character could not have a generation name. However, this is not so, for the sources refer to another type, called the 'part p'ai-hang'[51]. In the 'part p'ai-hang' the common element, the 'generation name', consists of only one part of the character, usually the radical.[52] This 'part p'ai-hang' is evidently rare and I have not to my knowledge encountered an example in Malaysia; but then I have never looked for it, and examples might well be found if they are sought.

Kiang Kang-Hu (1934, p.137) tells us how this began; he relates that in the Han Dynasty (beginning about 206BC), each clan in China held a meeting of its leaders to select a list of names which

---

[47] Bauer, 1957:598.

[48] Tzu[4] (G12,324) "A name or style taken at the age of 20".

[49] cf. Mathews (M4991) and Giles (G8780); Bauer (1957:597) challenges Mathews' translation.

[50] See Bauer, 1957:597-8.

[51] See Bauer, 1957:596-8.

[52] Van der Sprenkel, 1963:167 refers to the practice, but not specifically in generation names; as does Watson (1986:621-2).

would be adopted as the 'generation names' of subsequent generations of the clan. So that they could be more easily remembered, the names were arranged in the form of a poem, each line consisting of five names, and each stanza consisting of either two, four or six lines.

When a son is born in a Chinese family, the father ascertains from the clan association what the appropriate generation name is, and uses it as the first personal name of the son.

It is usual for each clan to have its own individual table of generation names, and it will be exclusive to those of that particular clan. To illustrate the use of generation names, given below is a list of the generation names which are actually being used by the Ang clan — my informant originated from Amoy in Hokkien Province. The complete list of names would be very long, and this is merely an extract of the part of the list which is in current use. The names are transcribed according to the Hokkien pronunciation, and the examples on the right are written in the form which would be most usually encountered. The generation names from 'Se' onwards are for future use.

Bun	文	e.g.	Ang Boon Beng
Kong	公	e.g.	Ang Kong Chian
Ho	候	e.g.	Ang Ho Yew
Se	世		
Tek	德		
Chiau	招		
Chu	資		
Lai	來		
Hu	許		

This particular branch of the Ang family reached the first name mentioned 文 about two generations ago, and the name Ang Boon Beng given as example on the right was the name of a man of that generation; all of his sons took the middle name 公 and all of his grandsons took the middle name 候; examples of their names are given too. When the last name in the current list has been reached, a further poem will be composed for the use of future generations, of course without repeating any name which has already been used.

Similarly each successive generation takes the appropriate generation name. Naturally it may happen that one branch of the family will be further down the table of names than will other branches, due to more rapid reproduction.

Maurice Freedman & Marjorie Topley note that when the members of certain religious communities in Singapore in the 1950s adopted kinship terms as if they were members of a "family", they adopted names including generation names.[53]

The question of 'generation names' of the Chinese is discussed comprehensively by Wolfgang Bauer in his article (1957) and his book (1959, pp.147-222).

Members of the Khoo 邱 Family Association of Cannon Square in Penang can obtain a printed list of the generation names (from the 8th to the 47th generations) from their association; it is reproduced below. The English version of the heading which it bears is:

"Genealogical Code Words for Members of Leong San Tong Khoo Kongsi who are the descendants of Khoo Chian Eng Kong of Sin Kang Seah, Sam Toh County, Hai Teng District, Chiang Chew Prefecture, Hokkien Province."[54]

When I visited the Leong San Tong Khoo Association in 1995, after an interval of forty years, an identical list (covering the 8th to the 47th generations) was still being handed out to members. Living Khoos belong to roughly the 21st generation.

For comparison I also append a copy of the list of generation names for the Sek Tong Siah Cheah Clan Association of Penang. It will be seen that this begins with the 1st generation, and concludes with the 40th.[55]

---

[53] Maurice Freedman & Marjorie Topley, 1961, p.21. However, these may have been religious "generation names" - see p.77 below.

[54] I plan to publish an article on the Chiangchew Hokkiens which will discuss these place names.

[55] Other writers mention shorter lists of generation names, e.g. Weig (1931:viii) writes of a sequence of twelve. Van der Sprenkel (1963:167) seems to visualise a cycle of only five generation names, each to be repeated every five generations; I find this puzzling.

Fig. 1: Generation names - Khoo clan

8th Generation 八世 圭 Kay	18th Generation 十八世 台 Thai	28th Generation 廿八世 一 It	38th Generation 卅八世 貽 Ee
9th Generation 九世 璧 Phaik	19th Generation 十九世 衡 Heng	29th Generation 廿九世 貫 Kuan	39th Generation 卅九世 謀 Boh
10th Generation 十世 呈 Theng	20th Generation 二十世 思 Soo	30th Generation 三十世 書 Soo	40th Generation 四十世 資 Choo
11th Generation 十一世 雲 Hoon	21st Generation 廿一世 繼 Kay	31st Generation 卅一世 紳 Sin	41st Generation 四十一世 燕 Ean
12th Generation 十二世 瑞 Swee	22nd Generation 廿二世 武 Boo	32nd Generation 卅二世 永 Aing	42nd Generation 四十二世 翼 Ek
13th Generation 十三世 人 Jin	23rd Generation 廿三世 鼎 Teng	33rd Generation 卅三世 千 Chian	43rd Generation 四十三世 世 Say
14th Generation 十四世 文 Boon	24th Generation 廿四世 甲 Kah	34th Generation 卅四世 秋 Chiew	44th Generation 四十四世 業 Giap
15th Generation 十五世 煥 Huan	25th Generation 廿五世 勵 Lay	35th Generation 卅五世 錫 Saik	45th Generation 四十五世 仰 Giang
16th Generation 十六世 國 Kok	26th Generation 廿六世 承 Sin	36th Generation 卅六世 福 Hock	46th Generation 四十六世 清 Cheng
17th Generation 十七世 華 Hua	27th Generation 廿七世 家 Kar	37th Generation 卅七世 遐 Har	47th Generation 四十七世 嘉 Kah

Fig. 2: Generation names - Cheah clan

1st Generation 一世 東 Tong	2nd Generation 二世 山 San	3rd Generation 三世 稱 Cheng	4th Generation 四世 重 Tiong	5th Generation 五世 望 Bong
6th Generation 六世 江 Kang	7th Generation 七世 左 Cho	8th Generation 八世 舊 Kiu	9th Generation 九世 家 Keh	10th Generation 十世 聲 Seng
11th Generation 十一世 世 Say	12th Generation 十二世 澤 Tek	13th Generation 十三世 千 Chian	14th Generation 十四世 年 Lian	15th Generation 十五世 久 Kiew
16th Generation 十六世 崇 Chong	17th Generation 十七世 揩 Kye	18th Generation 十八世 一 It	19th Generation 十九世 品 Phin	20th Generation 二十世 榮 Eng
21st Generation 廿一世 丕 Phi	22nd Generation 廿二世 承 Sin	23rd Generation 廿三世 惟 Ui	24th Generation 廿四世 祖 Chaw	25th Generation 廿五世 烈 Liat
26th Generation 廿六世 致 Ti	27th Generation 廿七世 恪 Khok	28th Generation 廿八世 在 Chye	29th Generation 廿九世 宗 Chong	30th Generation 三十世 枋 Peng
31st Generation 卅一世 百 Pek	32nd Generation 卅二世 代 Tye	33rd Generation 卅三世 源 Guan	34th Generation 卅四世 流 Liu	35th Generation 卅五世 遠 Uan
36th Generation 卅六世 芝 Chi	37th Generation 卅七世 蘭 Lan	38th Generation 卅八世 次 Chu	39th Generation 卅九世 第 Tay	40th Generation 四十世 生 Seng

A list of generation names used by a Mau (毛) lineage can be found in the book of Edward Seu Chen Mau.[56]

It seems that nowadays in Malaysia, generation names are no longer widely used, and then only by those who maintain contact with the clan association where they can have access to the list of generation names. I have been told that a higher proportion of

---

[56] Edward Seu Chen Mau, 1989:332-335.

Cantonese adhere to the practice. Some confirmation for this can be found in *The Mau Lineage* by Edward Seu Chen Mau, since the lineage seems to have its homeland in Kwangtung Province. He makes frequent mention of overseas members of the Mau clan who were acquainted with their generation names. But he does mention that the use of generation names in China itself was discontinued by the People's Republic of China from about 1966 on account of the Cultural Revolution.[57]

But writing of the Chinese in Sarawak in 1949, (where Cantonese were in a minority,) T'ien Ju-k'ang remarks "even the least literate peasant usually knows to which generation in the supposed clan genealogy he belongs".[58] He writes further specifically of members of the T'ien surname groups that they were aware of their generation status, and they referred to fellow clansmen accordingly as "uncles" or "aunts", or "nephews" or "nieces" as appropriate.[59] And even westernized Chinese in Malaysia recognize the custom; one Penang man told me: "If I meet a relative having my father's generation name, I address him as 'Uncle'".

It is quite usual however for any parents to give identical middle names to each of their sons, although this middle name may not be a generation name.

Some also confer on each of their daughters an identical middle name; but except in the case of Hakkas, the middle name chosen for the daughters of a family will be different from that chosen for the sons of the same family.

The order of seniority between brothers

According to the ancient Chinese *Book of Etiquette and Ceremonial*,[60] when an officer's son is 'capped' (a ritual carried out when he attains marriageable age) he is addressed by one of the

---

[57] Edward Seu Chen Mau, 1989:31-2,335.

[58] T'ien Ju-k'ang, 1956:22,26.

[59] T'ien Ju-k'ang, 1956:26,29.

[60] See Couvreur, 1916:21 and Steele, 1917 vol.1:15.

following terms, depending on whether he is first, second, third or youngest son in the family:

Son	Chinese	Mathews	Mandarin	Giles	CCC	Amoy
Eldest	伯	M4977	Pê^2	G9340	C0130	pek
Second	仲	M1505	Chung^4	G2876	C0112	tiöng
Third	叔	M5881	Shu^2	G10,039	C0647	siok
Youngest	季	M435	Chi^4	G944	C1323	kùi

These four characters are defined as "four characters used for denoting the first, second, third, and fourth, of brothers".[61] These forms are also used in formal language to address an ancestor when offerings are being made, according to whether the ancestor was eldest, second, third or fourth of the brothers in his family.

We saw[62] that one term used for the 'generation name' is 'p'ai hang', or more precisely 'p'ai hang tzu' 排行字. Similarly the 'p'ai hang' denoting the seniority between brothers, that is seniority in age *within* one generation, can be denoted precisely with the term

排行順   p'ai^2 hang^2 shun^4 [63]   pâi hâng sün

This 'p'ai hang shun' plays a much less important role than the 'generations p'ai-hang', and I have not heard of these names being used in this way in Malaya.

The Second Given Name (the last name)

At first sight this is just a personal name, chosen at random by the parents of a child. Sometimes it will have a discernable association of meaning with the first given name, whether that be a generation name or not; the father who chose this name for his son obviously was inviting prosperity:

---

[61] Giles no.9340. Also see Bauer, 1957:597.

[62] on page 13.

[63] It is discussed by Bauer, 1957:598-603, and Bauer, 1959:153-163. For the meaning of p'ai^2 see M4870, G8579; for hang^2 M2754(c), G4624; for shun^4 M5935, G10,143.

黃來幅	Ng Lai Hock	(Ng – the Surname)
		(Lai – to come)
		(Hock – prosperity)

Similarly, no doubt, the father who chose this name:

黃速利	Ng Sok Lee	(Ng – the Surname)
		(Sok – quick)
		(Lee – gain)

It sometimes happens, though rarely, that this last name is a generation name, and the middle name will then, of course be a personal name.[64]

For example, there are four Cantonese brothers, called:

陳富山	Chan Foo San
陳貴山	Chan Kwee San
陳榮山	Chan Weng San
陳華山	Chan Hwa San

The generation name of these brothers is 山 (in Mandarin *shan*), meaning 'hill'.

Chinese often use great ingenuity, and artistry, in the choice of names for their children, and it will sometimes be found, for instance, that the personal names of the sons of a family when read in sequence give a rhyme or common saying. In the example above the personal names read in sequence (Foo Kwee Weng Hwa) comprise a recognized Chinese saying (which may be found embroidered on curtains and the like) meaning literally "Wealth-honour-glory-splendour".

Variation: one personal name only
Some people have a surname and one personal name only, for instance: 黃結 Wong Keat, a Cantonese man (Wong being the surname); and 呂甜 Loo Tee, a Hokkien woman (Loo likewise being the surname). This custom, simple enough in itself, is worth

---

[64] Lin Shan (1994:11) states "The generation names may be used as the first or second word in a two-character name". My impression is that it is rarely the second word, but it is sometimes: Edward Mau (1989:31) cites examples of its use in both first and second positions, without comment.

pursuing for the valuable light it throws on the relative functions of the first and second personal names.

De Groot observes "Before and during the Tsin Dynasty names of one character were the rule, and those of two characters exceptional, but after that we see names of two characters slowly increase, till during the Ming Dynasty, as at present, their number manifestly exceeds that of the others"[65].

Such a single-character personal name is known in Chinese as 單名 Tan[1] ming[2] (*Amoy* Tan mia^n). 'Tan' has such meanings as 'single', 'odd' and 'alone', which can have distasteful connotations in traditional Chinese belief. At all events there is a belief current amongst Hokkien Chinese at least,[66] that to have one personal name is in some sense inferior to having two personal names; to remedy this, a Hokkien having only one personal name may resort to the device of employing the word 文 (*Mand.* Wen, *Amoy* Bun) meaning 'elegant' or 'refined', as a middle name. For example, a Hokkien man whose name originally was 陳榜 Tan Pong later appeared as 陳文榜 Tan Boon Pong.

The special significance of the second given name

It will not have escaped the reader that the word 'Boon' used to "fill in" occupies the middle position of the three-part name, and the existing personal name remains in the last position. The function of this last name will repay further examination. In my 1959 publication (p.19) I wrote, without attaching much importance to the matter: "It may be that in some Chinese personal names the last name is really looked upon as being the name of the individual, and the middle name is merely a descriptive word which qualifies the personal name." Further research leads me to the view that this is in fact the case, and further reflection leads me to the view that (contrary to my belief then) it is of considerable significance to our understanding of the function of personal names.

---

[65] De Groot, 1910, Vol.6, p.1134.

[66] Said to be not known to the Cantonese, but see p.29 below.

21

The clue to this matter turned up in a footnote in a German publication on Chinese names, citing the French scholar H. Maspero.[67] Maspero reported that in early documents from the T'ang Dynasty, he found that some officials signed with both characters of their personal names, and others signed with the second character only. But very significantly, *none signed with the first character only*. Maspero's conclusion was that at that time, it was the second of the two which was the true personal name, and the first was little more than an auspicious character separating the family name and the personal name. This appeals to me as having general validity.

It at once throws light on several aspects of the naming system. For example, if the second personal name is the important one, we can understand how (with rare exceptions) it is the first personal name which can become the generation name, shared with others; and we can see why it is usually the first personal name which is sometimes replaced with 'Ah' or 'Bun'; in both cases the second personal name is left inviolate as the individual's real name. We shall see other examples to illustrate this point: (see for example 'marriage names' on p.88). It may have a syntactical angle too: is the relative importance of the last name due to the fact that the first personal name often has an adjectival function, and the last name is a noun?

The Five Elements

According to a popular Chinese Taoist belief, the universe is made up of five elements which are:

Chinese	In Mandarin	In Hokkien	Translation
金	Chin	Kim	Gold (or metal)
木	Mu	Bok	Wood
水	Shui	Sui	Water
火	Huo	Ho^{n}	Fire
土	T'u	Tho	Earth

---

[67] Bauer, 1959:116.

When a child is born its parents, if they are inclined toward conservative belief, will consult an astrologer who, after reference to the child's date of birth and to his own almanacs, will advise whether the child is likely to be deficient in any of the five elements. If his findings show that the child would be in fact deficient in one or two of the elements, then the deficiency will be made good by the choice of names consisting of those elements.

The following names, quite common amongst the old fashioned, may be given as examples of such personal names:

Chinese	In Mandarin	In Hokkien	Translation
水火	Shui Huo	Chui He	'Water & fire'
水土	Shui T'u	Chui Tho	'Water & earth'
土水	T'u Shui	Tho Chui	'Earth & water'

More sophisticated people will not use the simple name of the deficient element, but will choose a name which, when written in Chinese, contains the character of the element,[68] e.g.

Chinese	In Mandarin	In Hokkien	Translation
(a) 錦江	Chin Chiang	Gim Kang	'Elegant river'

(The first character 錦 contains the 'Gold' radical 金; The second character contains the 'Water' radical 水 written 氵 see p.47 note 3).

	In Mandarin	In Hokkien	Translation
(b) 木森	Mu Shen	Bak Sim	'Wood & luxuriant vegetation'

(Both words contain 'wood' 木)

Given below are some names, of actual persons, which serve as illustrations of this custom of including the elements in the names of children:

Chinese	In Mandarin	In Own dialect	Translation
林木林	Lin Mu Lin	Lim Bak Lim	Surname - 'timber' - 'forest'

---

[68] De Groot attributes the use of a character containing the radical of the element, in preference to the simple character of the element, to cases where the astrologer advises that the simple character of the element would work too strongly (De Groot, 1910, Vol.6, p.1136).

(Note how the 'wood' element occurs five times in his name)

李水金	Li Shui Chin	Lee Chooi Kim	Surname - 'water' - 'gold'
駱火土	Lo Huo T'u	Lok Hua Thor	Surname - 'fire' - 'earth'
		(A Teochew labourer)	
李土水	Li T'u Shui	Lee Thor Sooi	Surname - 'earth' - 'water'

In a book published in 1876, N.B. Dennys[69] reproduces a facsimile of a Chinese charm relating to the birth of a boy in Canton in 1872. After noting the date and hour of birth, the document goes on to predict the fate of the boy at various periods of his life; then comes a paragraph advising the parents that he should adopt the Kum-fa goddess as his spiritual mother, that he should be shaved at a certain time, and that he should be a year old before he was vaccinated; this part of the document includes the words: "In selecting a name for him some character should be chosen having *To* (土), earth, as a component part. It will then be lucky."

It is not stated whether this advice was followed, (possibly it was not, as it is related that the boy died while still young).[70] Cobbold relates that each of the five elements is presided over by a deity, and describes how the task of Chinese physicians is "to ascertain which of the five elements is preponderating, and then to counteract its influence by proper antidotes".[71] The comprehensive discussion of the topic by Evelyn Lip, who devotes a chapter to the influence of the five elements, is evidence of the continuing lively interest in this subject.[72]

---

[69] Dennys, 1876:53-54

[70] The incorporation of the five elements in the choice of names is discussed by Bauer, 1959:183-89, 239-45; and by Williams, 1932:184-5 .

[71] Cobbold, 1988:33-34.

[72] Evelyn Lip, 1994:2-28, also 103-4.

The Animal Cycle and personal names

Lin Shan and Evelyn Lip[73] list the radicals and words which according to Chinese belief should be selected for personal names depending on the year of the 12-year animal cycle the child was born in. The animals are rat, ox, tiger, hare, dragon, snake, horse, goat, monkey, cock, dog and pig.

In ancient China, (from the sixth century BC,) prominent persons were sometimes given names such as "dragon" or "tiger" or "horse" derived from the year of their birth in the animal cycle. The practice was in use in AD500. "among people of nomadic origin living on the northern frontier of China". An instance is given of a nomadic chief born in AD296 (a tiger year), who had 'Tiger' incorporated in his name. Some names were avoided: '"Dog" became early a term of abuse, "hare" usually connotes lewdness, "pig" wildness and grossness of character.[74]

Numbers in names

In the last century it seems that officials were sometimes named with numbers, such as 八十八 "88" and 七十五 "75". G.M.H. Playfair writes "There was a Manchu official at Amoy some years ago named similarly 八十四 ["84"]. I have heard that such names are given (always to Bannermen, I believe,) as a record of the age attained by their grandmothers at the time they were born."[75] Such fancies are unknown in Malaysia.

In common with other societies, the Chinese sometimes name their children, after the first, by numbers (e.g. number two, number three and so on).

To illustrate this, given below are the names of a Hakka family (surnamed 'Chin'):

	Chinese	Spelt	Translation
Eldest son	陳大仔	Chin Tai Chai	(surname-big-son)
Eldest daughter	陳大妹	Chin Tai Moy	(surname-big-daughter)
Second son	陳二仔	Chin Nee Chai	(surname-two-son)

---

[73] Lin Shan, 1994:145-152; Evelyn Lip, 1994:117-119.

[74] Boodberg, 1938:247,252; Boodberg, 1939:273-5; Boodberg, 1940:133,135.

[75] In *China Review* 17, 1888-89:240.

Third son	陳三仔	Chin Sam Chai	(surname-three-son)
Second daughter	陳二妹	Chin Nee Moy	(surname-two-daughter)
Fourth son	陳四仔	Chin See Chai	(surname-four-son)
Fifth (and youngest son)	陳滿仔	Chin Man Chai	(surname-full-son)

Note to the above:

(i) It will be noticed that the first child is not called 'One' (written in Chinese (一), but the word for 'Big' (大) is used instead.

(ii) The word Chai 仔 is a diminutive word, which also means 'son'. It is often used as a name by Fuichiu and Teochew Hakkas, and sometimes by Kayengchew Hakkas and Teochews.

(iii) The word Moy 妹 is generally held to mean 'Younger sister', but it is commonly used as a name for girls by the Hakkas and Cantonese. In Taiphoo, it is used only in the sense of 'Younger sister', and is not given as name to daughters. In Hokchew it is used as a name for daughters, and even sometimes as a name for sons. But of course there are other names spelt similarly in English which do not represent the character 妹; for example there is a young Hokchew man called U Yong Moi 余養梅 where the character for Moi is 梅 meaning 'Plums'.

(iv) The name 'Man' 滿 (meaning 'Full') is given to a child when it is hoped that that child will be the last to be born to the parents.

And here are two more examples, giving actual names which include a number:

Chinese	Spelling	Translation
岑亞二	Shum Ah Yee	Shum: The surname
		Ah: a familiar word;
	(A Cantonese woman)	Yee: 'Two'
		(She is probably the second daughter in the family).
周三妹	Chow Sam Mooi	Chow: The surname
	(A Hakka woman)	Sam: 'Three'
		Mooi: 'Daughter'
		(She is probably the third daughter in the family).

Some examples

In illustration of some of the points mentioned so far, given below is a table of the names of a whole family from the Hokkien Province, (spelling being that in common use, not strictly phonetic):

Husband	黃廷華	Ng Teng Hoa
Wife	陳刊治	Tan Khan Tee
Daughter	黃秀月	Ng Siew Goat
Daughter	黃秀美	Ng Siew Bee
Daughter	黃秀葉	Ng Siew Heoh
Son	黃來幅	Ng Lai Hock
Son	黃來文	Ng Lai Boon
Son	黃萊發	Ng Lai Hoat
Daughter	黃秀冠	Ng Siew Khwan
Daughter	黃秀英	Ng Siew Eng

Possibly the name 'Lai' given to each of the sons is a generation name, but the information provided here is not sufficient to put the matter beyond doubt.

In the same vein, Creamer cites the case of Mao Tse Tung the Chinese leader and his two brothers, who bore the names:

Chinese	Mandarin	Pinyin
毛澤東	Mao Che Tung	Mao Zedong
毛澤民	Mao Che Min	Mao Zemin
毛澤覃	Mao Che T'an	Mao Zetan[76]

And we may consider the names of a Hakka family, illustrating the custom among Hakka people of giving an identical middle name to both sons and daughters:

	In Chinese	Hakka Pronunciation
Husband	何生民	Ho Sang Man
Wife	吳雪英	Ng Saik Jing
Son	何思志	Ho Soo Chee
Daughter	何思娥	Ho Soo Ngo

---

[76] Creamer, 1995:911. 'Ze' means "luster, beneficence". This may or may not be a generation name.

Daughter	何思麗	Ho Soo Lee
Son	何思吉	Ho Soo Keat
Son	何思文	Ho Soo Boon

(The middle name for each son and daughter being 思 Soo).

The names of all the sons in a Hakka family given below show how there is sometimes an association of meaning between the two personal names; in this case, the name Li (a Chinese mile) was chosen for the sons by the grandfather, (it may or may not have been the generation name given by the clan association); the parents have then chosen for each son a middle name which combines with it to give a meaning:

In Chinese	Hakka pronunciation	In English
林萬里	Lim Man Li	Ten thousand miles
林千里	Lim Chien Li	One thousand miles
林百里	Lim Pah Li	One hundred miles
林十里	Lim Sip Li	Ten miles
林九里	Lim Kow Li	Nine miles

In contrast with the limited number of surnames in use, a list of the words which are in use in Malaya as personal names will include well over three thousand.

The choice of a name seems to be more often influenced by the meaning of the word than by the sound. It is natural that agreeable and flattering names (such as elegant, precious, excellent) should be most commonly used, but, as is remarked later in these notes, very unpleasant words are sometimes used too.

II Variations in the Form of Names

The basic form of Chinese names was considered in the previous section; before going further we may look at some of the common variations.

The use of Ah (亞 or 阿)
This word of indeterminate meaning[1] occurs very commonly as the first personal name of Chinese, (particularly in the names of Cantonese and Hakkas), being used in front of the last personal name; for example, a Hakka woman whose full name is:

黄三妹 Wong Sam Moi may be known familiarly as 亞妹 Ah Moi.

De Groot writes[2] "Monosyllabic names are in some parts of China, for instance Canton, preceded with obvious frequency by the word 亞 or 阿, 'A' or 'O', which, being apparently meaningless, is often omitted in writing." It has been suggested already (see p.21) that the Cantonese do not share the Hokkien apprehension that one personal name is inferior to two personal names; but one has to wonder whether in this instance it would be more accurate to see the 'Ah' — a virtually meaningless particle — as being inserted in informal speech to fill a perceived gap,

---

[1] The Chinese Encyclopaedic Dictionary (*Tz'u Hai*) attributes to it the meaning of secondary, e.g. 亞父 — secondary father; in Chinese names its significance, insofar as it has any significance, may be a blend of affection and contempt and familiarity. Either of the two characters 亞 and 阿 may be used for 'Ah'; the former is much more commonly used, the latter being considered archaic by Hokkiens, seldom used by Kheks, and never used by Cantonese in Malaysia — its usual pronunciation in Cantonese is 'Oh' rather than 'Ah'.

[2] De Groot, 1910, VI:1135.

rather than as a formal part of the name which is omitted in writing. This view would seem to find support in the remark of Dyer Ball quoted below.

Bauer[3] discusses the use of 'Ah' in the South Chinese dialects, citing S.W. Williams[4]: "In Canton and its vicinity the names of people are abbreviated in conversation to one character, and a 'A' prefixed to it, as Tsin-teh called A-teh, or A-tsin. In Amoy the 'A' is placed after, as Chin-a; in the northern provinces no such usage is known." Regarding the usage in the "northern provinces", 'Ah' was in fact in use in Peking in the 1950s.

Dyer Ball (writing about milk names) observes[5] "This name of infancy often consists of but one character, and in that case has, in the extreme South, the prefix 'Ah' put before it, so that a boy named Ch'un Luk will commonly be called Ch'un Ah Luk, though the 'Ah' is not really a part of his name. In the Fuh-keen so-called dialects, this 'Ah' is not used."

The Chinese characters 亞 and 阿 cannot be used as surnames, and, with certain very rare exceptions which can be ignored for practical purposes, the spelling 'A' and 'Ah' cannot represent any Chinese surname. This generalisation is of some value to anyone dealing with records of Chinese names, since it eliminates the risk of a name being indexed under this common form 'Ah' in mistake for a surname.

As a matter of interest, I have on one or two occasions seen the name Au — 歐 the first part of Au-Iong mentioned on page 10 — spelt 'Ah'; this is no doubt a spelling error, since it does not represent any of the various pronunciations of the Chinese character.

It may also be mentioned that, in a list of surnames included in the Amoy Romanized Dictionary by the Rev. W. Campbell,[6] the following surnames are mentioned:

---

[3] Bauer (1959:143)

[4] From S.W. Williams, 1883. *The Middle Kingdom*, 1, 798.

[5] Dyer Ball, 1900:397.

[6] Campbell, 1913:1048. The CCC numbers are 4102 and 0686 respectively; see Appendix B.

Chinese	Mandarin	Romanized Hokkien as given by Campbell
百	Pai	Ah
向	Hsiang	A^n

I find it difficult to believe that either of these surnames would ever be encountered in Malaysia with these spellings. One other instance — I have seen the spelling 'Ah' used for the Teochew pronunciation of the surname 夏 Hsia; it is more usual for the spelling 'Hah' to be used however.

As S.W. Williams suggested, amongst the Hokkien and Teochew communities it is rather less usual for the word 'Ah' to be used in front of a given name in familiar matters. It is more usual for a man to be known by the last name only, e.g. Lean Teong Sim may be known to his intimates as Sim, or sometimes Sim-A.

Another useful generalization may be made here:

'Ah' will seldom be found as the last part of a Chinese name, (i.e. in place of the second personal name, in a name with three characters). Thus, if you see a name written like this, the overwhelming probability is that the surname is that part of the name which immediately precedes 'Ah':

Chooi, Cheong Ah

either Chooi or Cheong can represent surnames; if it had been written Chooi, Ah Cheong then it could have been deduced that Chooi was the surname, and a comma had been put after it in error; but written Chooi, Cheong Ah as above, one can fairly confidently say that the surname is Cheong, and the full name is Cheong Ah Chooi, and that it has been written in this odd way by someone, accustomed to European names, who has taken the last name Chooi to be the surname, and brought it to the front for index purposes. Indeed, Western library cataloguers usually give the name in the conventional order, surname first, but with a comma after the surname as here.

But there are always exceptions;[7] for example, I have seen the name of an elderly Henghwa woman written thus:

王前亞 Wang Chuen Ah

And in China these personal names could be chosen to express a national aspiration:

建亞   Chien Ya meaning "Build up Asia".

Such exceptions are rarely encountered; it is possible that on occasion confusion arises between the character 亞 and a character pronounced similarly, 仔 a diminutive which at the end of a name would mean 'the second'. (c.f. page 26, note ii).

The familiar form 'Ah' may be used in place of the first given name even when the surname is used also, e.g.:

林亞妹 Lim Ah Moy   (Name of a Teochew woman)
黃亞妹 Wong Ah Moy   (Name of a Cantonese or Hakka
                     woman)
林亞九 Lim Ah Kow   (Name of a Hokkien man)

This use of 'Ah' in place of the first given name is fairly common in fact, and for example a Hokkien man called:

陳大頭 Tan Twa Thow (Literally 'Big-headed Tan')

may be called by his friends, and even known in official matters as

陳亞頭 Tan Ah Thow   (The 'Ah', as already mentioned,
                     having no distinct meaning of its
                     own).

Sometimes people are better known by the 'Ah' form than by their real name; for example the nineteenth century pioneer in

---

[7] C.S. Wong quotes another case too — Tan Chin Ah (陳振亞), formerly the editor of the *Kwong Wah Jit Po* in Penang.

Selangor is always known to history as Yap Ah Loy, rather than by his full name which was Yap Tet Loy.[8]

It is rare to find the familiar 'Ah' in the names of people who have received their education in Chinese schools in Malaysia, since any child who used this name at the time of entry to the school would be given a more seemly and significant name by the teacher. But it does not follow that everyone having 'Ah' in his name is uneducated, since Chinese who have been educated in English schools often retain this form throughout their life, even though they may become highly educated professional men; for example I can think off-hand of at least two judges in Malaysia who retain 'Ah' as a middle name.[9]

In spite of assertions to the contrary, it is a fact that this 'Ah' will sometimes be found in the names of Chinese resident in China.

Other ways of writing names

In informal matters the surname of a Chinese may be omitted, and only the given names used to identify him. For example, a Hakka man called

Yew Kim Seong ('Yew' being the surname) may be called by his friends:

Kim Seong, or 'Mr. Kim Seong'.

It is inevitable that the names shown in official records sometimes take this form too, omitting the surname, and when a name consisting of two words only is encountered it is often difficult to decide whether the two words are both given names (the surname having been omitted), or whether the first is a surname and the second a given name.

---

[8] Yap Ah Loy was born in Kwangtung Province in 1837. Although he was also known as Yap Mao Lan his real name was Yap Tet Loy. He died in Kuala Lumpur in 1885.

[9] Mr Blythe drew my attention to another possibility, namely Mr Lee Ah Soo, whose middle name was 雅, a word which can be pronounced 'Ah' in Cantonese.

If the father's name is also known, comparison of the first word of each name will generally settle the matter: if the first word of each is identical, this may be assumed to be the surname, since surnames are hereditary among the Chinese, and (as explained on pp.91-94, below) it is extremely rare for any given-names of parent and child to be identical. If the Chinese characters of the names are not known it is less easy to settle the point, but the western spelling does give a fairly reliable indication generally. For instance, a Chinese woman has an identity card showing her name as Lay Yin daughter of Hoe Heng. Even though the Chinese characters are not known, it is fairly obvious that the Lay of the daughter and the Hoe of the father cannot represent identical names, and that therefore the name is incorrectly shown. In this case it was found on inquiry that the daughter's full name was Hoe Lay Yin daughter of Hoe Heng.

Some Chinese follow the western convention when writing their names, and write the surname last, after the personal name. For example, a man called Lim Hen Peng (the surname being Lim) may choose to be known as Hen Peng Lim; some indeed go further in their adherence to western custom, and use only the initials of the personal names, so that Lim Hen Peng might style himself "H.P. Lim"; and there are even people who write their names in the conventional Chinese order, with the surname first, but substitute the initial letters for the surname and first personal name, so that the name mentioned might be written L.H. Peng, so obscuring the surname altogether. Mercifully, such people are not numerous.[10]

Nowadays it is quite usual to find the two personal names written together (as Lim Henpeng), which makes it clear that the last two elements are the personal names[11]. As we have seen, in

---

[10] It was reported from the Netherlands Indies as early as 1917 that many Chinese had begun writing their names in the European manner, e.g. M. L. Oei in place of Oei Moo Liem, with the family name being written last. *Encyclopaedie van Nederlandsch-Indië*, 1, 487, (The Hague/Leiden).

[11] This manner of writing the name has been used, and urged, by Chinese for a long time. See for example Lin Yutang (he was a Chiangchew Hokkien) *My Country and my People* (London: Wm Heinemann), 1936:348.

library catalogues, in conformity with the treatment of western names, it is the practice to insert a comma after the surname thus: Lim, Hen Peng. Other Chinese may insert a hyphen between the personal names, so that Lim Hen Peng becomes Lim Hen-Peng, or Hen-Peng Lim, and in either fashion it is clear which are the personal names and which is the surname.

But a word of caution is needed here: Chinese two-character surnames are often joined with a hyphen, so that the name Au Yang Yin quoted as an example on page 11 could equally well be written Au-Yang Yin. In practice the possible confusion between hyphenated two-character surnames and hyphenated personal names placed before the surname is more apparent than real, because one soon learns to recognize the few two-character surnames in common use, those apart from 歐陽 Au-Yang, 司徒 Szu-T'u and 司馬 Szu-Ma being very rarely encountered. In case of doubt reference to the list of surnames in Appendix B should indicate whether the name being considered is a two-character surname or not.

Probably the ideal way of writing a name in the Wade-Giles system is to stick to the conventional order with the surname first, to join the personal names with a hyphen, and to use a capital letter for the first personal name but a small letter for the second personal name; thus our example becomes:

Lim Hen-peng.

When names are written in Pinyin, generally the two personal names are written together, e.g.

李如龍 Li Rulong. But a professor in China who bears this name prefers to write them separately, in the form Li Ru Long.

Chinese Christians

Christian Chinese may use Christian names in addition to their Chinese names. For example, a man called Cheng Yu Tek has in addition the Christian name John. He may be known by any of the following:

(a) Cheng Yu Tek (i.e. his Chinese name only); or
(b) John Cheng (i.e. his Christian name and Chinese surname); or

(c) John Cheng Yu Tek (i.e. his Christian name followed by his full Chinese name).

Chinese Christians sometimes give Christian names to their children at birth, but others prefer to give ordinary Chinese names with no Christian significance. In the latter event, there is no way of knowing from the name whether it refers to a Christian or not.

Many Christian names have an accepted form of transcription into Chinese; for example, John in Chinese becomes:

Chinese	*Mandarin*	*Hokkien*
約翰	Yo-Han	Iok-Han ('Yo': a covenant; 'Han': a pencil — imitation of the sound only)

An English-educated Christian will generally use the English form, and a Chinese educated person will use the Chinese form; for example, a man with the surname Chuah may be known to his English acquaintances as 'John Chuah' and to his Chinese acquaintances as 'Chuah Iok Han'.

Chinese Christian names are chosen mostly from the New Testament and, to conform with the Chinese practice, those names which will transcribe into two syllables will be preferred; occasionally a three-syllable name will be used however — one such name is Timothy, which is transcribed:

Chinese	*Mandarin*	*Hokkien*
提摩太	Ti-Mo-T'ai	The-Mo-Thai

A Christian name given to a child at birth may be changed to a 'School name' (see p.85, below) later in life, just as any other name may.

In the event of an adult Chinese being converted to Christianity he will not as a rule change his name to a Christian name.[12]

---

[12] A British Christian missionary at Amoy wrote in 1876 that they did not recommend that converts change their Chinese names "unless the original name have something positively bad about it" (Letter from Carstairs Douglas dated Amoy, 9 December 1876, now in United Reformed Church Archives, London).

It is not unusual for non-Christian Chinese to adopt western names too, particularly cabaret singers and so on. There is a young Hokkien woman whose name is 宋露絲 - Rosy Song.

Sometimes a Chinese will use a western name and a Chinese name which are translations of each other, (rather than transcriptions imitating the sound); for example, a woman whose name in Chinese is 李寶珠 — written Lee Poh Choo (Lee being the surname, 'Poh' meaning 'precious' and 'Choo' meaning 'pearl') may choose to be known in English as 'Pearl Lee'.

Nowadays (in the 1990s) it is usual for Chinese students of English language in universities in China to adopt western names in addition to their Chinese names; to take two examples of students from Fujian Province:

Chinese	Mandarin	Hokkien (Amoy)
廖寧	Andy Liao Ning	Liä u Lê ng
黃樵夫	Susan Huang Qiaofu	Ng Chiâ u hû

A list of the more popular western names used by Chinese, with the most usual form of transcription of each, will be found in Appendix G.

Chinese Muslims

Islamic tradition has it that the first envoy from the Islamic Caliphate was sent to China in as early as AD651 by the Caliph Uthman. What is more certain is that Muslim Arab and Persian merchants had arrived in China by the eighth century AD (during the Tang Dynasty). They were maritime traders, and made permanent settlements at Chinese ports; there they were allowed to practise their religion with little interference. Canton became the home of a thriving Muslim trading community. In Hokkien Province the port of Chuanchew (Quanzhou) became the site for a Muslim trading settlement in the ninth century, and from the tenth to the thirteenth centuries was one of the most famous ports in China; it was known to the Arabs as Zaitun.

That is of particular interest to historians of the Nanyang. But the point has been made that a much greater contribution to the settled Muslim population in China was made by the incursion of

Muslims overland from the west.[13] One such accretion occurred when Muslim commanders and soldiers were introduced into China by the Mongol conquerors during the Yuan Dynasty (A.D. 1280-1368). Under the succeeding Ming and Ch'ing dynasties the Muslims became Sinicised in language and appearance; this was especially so in the cities. However, they always felt themselves apart from the Han Chinese. Since then in China, Islam has remained as the faith of a powerful minority group. It is found particularly in the Mongol and Turkish areas, and in the northern, northwestern and southwestern regions of China. Most Chinese Muslims belong to the Hanafi school of Islam.

Under the Republic, the Muslims were regarded as one of the five major ethnic groups of China (the others being Han Chinese, Manchu, Mongol and Tibetan) and in the Nationalist flag, in use from 1912 to 1928, the Muslims ('Hui')[14], were represented by the white horizontal stripe.

Establishing the total number of Muslims in China has been fraught with difficulty, and widely differing figures have been given; the main obstacle is that the censuses in China do not have a category for religion, and therefore precise figures cannot be given for the numbers of any religious group. The censuses do enumerate the "minority nationalities", and a reasonably reliable figure can be arrived at by calculating the total inhabitants in ten of these for which Islam is the prevailing religion.[15] Using data from the 1982 census in China, Barbara Pillsbury concludes "that 'about 14 million' is the number of Muslims on the Chinese mainland *according to official figures.*"[16]

It is not known how many Chinese have been converted to Islam in Malaya; many of these converts (*muallaf*) abandon their Chinese names altogether and assume Muslim names, so that they

---

[13] Yusuf Chang, 1981:30.

[14] See Mathews no.7187. But for a discussion of 'Hui', see Barbara Pillsbury, 1981:46-52.

[15] See Barbara Pillsbury, 1981. This depends on the assumption that they are Muslims by descent, not as a result of proselytization.

[16] Barbara Pillsbury, 1983, 4:231.

tend to become assimilated with the Malay population, and accordingly they pass outside the scope of this study.

The Chinese Muslim population which has brought its Muslim faith with it from China, on the other hand, preserves its Chinese identity more closely; its members seldom intermarry with Malays, and they preserve their Chinese names which they use alongside Muslim names, such as Ahmad, Musa, Mustapha, etc. They are of the Hanafi school of Islam.

I have no up-to-date figures for the total number of Chinese Muslims in Malaysia. At the census of 1931, 3,443 Chinese were returned as Muslims out of a total Chinese population in Malaya of 1,709,392 .[17] There is no way of establishing how many of these were *muallaf* and how many derived their Islam from China.

In course of time many of the Muslims who settled in China adopted Chinese names. When transcribing foreign names into their language, the Chinese endeavour to represent each syllable of the name with a Chinese word of similar sound; this is not so simple with Muslim names which consist usually of at least four syllables, often more (e.g. Abu Hasan, Abdul Rahman, Siti Fatimah, Muhammad Sulaiman, etc.), not to mention the father's name, preceeded by 'bin', which is often added to the personal name.[18]

To conform to Chinese custom, if possible the initial syllable will be the surname. A considerable number of the common Muslim names begins with 'M' (e.g. Muhammad, Mustapha, Malik), and as a result a large proportion of the Chinese Muslims have adopted the surname 馬 (Ma in Mandarin) which was used to transcribe this initial 'Ma', 'Mu', etc.; it has been estimated that 75% of the persons in China with this surname are Muslims, and it is a surname common also in the Muslim community in Malaysia.

Another common surname among Chinese Muslims was 蒲 'P'u'. We have record of a Muslim in Chuanchew in the Sung Dynasty whose surname was 'P'u'. Chau Ju-Kua records that in

---

[17] Purcell, 1948:127.

[18] This was discussed by Prof. S. Q. Fatimi in a paper delivered at the Conference of Southeast Asian Historians, Singapore, in January 1961.

thirteenth-century San-fo-ts'i (Palembang, Sumatra) "A large proportion of the people of this country are surnamed P'u". 'P'u' is probably the Chinese rendering of 'Bu', short for 'Abu' ("father" in Arabic, a frequent element in names).[19]

MARRIED WOMEN — Use of own and husbands' name

Under the established custom of southern China (but not often in Malaysia) a woman after marriage puts the surname of her husband before her full maiden name; for example, if a Miss Lim Mooi Lan marries a man named Tan Beng Choon she may be known after the marriage as:

陳林美蘭   Tan Lim Mooi Lan

Sometimes indeed, though again not commonly in Malaysia, a woman may be known after marriage by the husband's surname and the title 'Mrs.', in the western manner; so that our Miss Lim Mooi Lan after her marriage might instead be known as:

Chinese	Mandarin	Hokkien	English
陳太太	Ch'en Tai-Tai	Tan Thai Thai	Mrs. Tan

A dictionary definition of 太太 T'ai T'ai is "wife of an official; a lady; Mrs." Its use in the last sense is very common; it often follows the husband's surname, less often being used after his full name, and never after the maiden name of a woman; exceptionally, it may be used in a rather familiar manner following the *given names* of the husband only.

However, it is far more usual for a woman to retain her name unchanged after marriage. The continued use of individual surnames after marriage was considered of sufficient importance to merit the inclusion of the following provision in the Marriage Law of the People's Republic of China, promulgated in 1950, (Article 11): "Both husband and wife shall have the right to use his or her own family name."

---

[19] Hirth & Rockhill, 1911:16,60,64.

Married Women — Use of 'Shih'

The word 氏 'Shih' (*Pinyin* 'Shi') has an interesting history. Kiang Kang-hu writes[20] that in ancient times "two classes of family names were in use, the first called Shih (氏), being an hereditary title from the father side given by and held at the pleasure of the emperor, king, or lord. This class of name was used by men only. The other class was called Hsing (姓), to indicate the origin of birth from the mother side; this second class was used by both men and women."

In later times there has been a curious reversal of the function of these two words: The Hsing (*Pinyin* 'xing') has come to be passed down the male line; and 'Shih' is attached specifically to the names of women, having acquired the meaning 'née'. [21]

Giles[22] writes about Shih: 'Originally the family name: a family; a clan. Used in petitions by women, of themselves', e.g. '羅氏. The Lo family or clan'; and '黃門李氏 or 黃李氏 Mrs. Huang née Li'. In Malaysia I have never seen an instance of a name written like that just quoted, employing the character 門 (except on gravestones, where it is quite common).

But the use of 氏 Shih with the surname only is quite usual with married Chinese women, particularly those of advancing years. It is often translated 'Madam', and as we see it is used after the woman's own surname, not her husband's. For example, Miss Lim might be known after her marriage as:

Chinese	Mandarin	Hokkien	English
林氏	Lin Shih	Lim Si	Madam Lim

It may happen that a woman will be known in this fashion from early-in life, and that her children may never discover what

---

[20] 1934:126; on this point see also Wojtasiewicz, 1954:23-26; and Creamer, 1995:909.

[21] But not exclusively — Edward Mau (1989:359) gives the name of a Mau surname association starting with 'Mau See ...' (毛氏) "The Mau clan ..."

[22] No.9978.

her personal names are; this is especially probable if she belongs to the middle class.[23]

For example, I saw an application for an entry permit for Malaya in respect of a 34-year-old Hainanese lady in China. The application was by her husband, who one would expect to have known her actual name. But her name was given simply as "Lee Tee" 李氏.

The use of 'Shih' is in fact particularly common in respect of Hainanese women though it is also practised by Teochews and others; the word 氏 in Hainanese is generally pronounced 'Tee'. Three further examples are given below, retaining the spelling of the name as pronounced in Hainanese:

Tan Tee	陳氏
Wee Tee	黃氏
Yeo Tee	揚氏

(See also the note on the use of 女士 Nu Shih under 'Titles' on p.105, below).

The two examples of the names of married couples (Hainanese), at first sight seem to indicate conflict with the generally accepted rule that men and women with the same surname should not intermarry, (See pp.101-104 below); but in fact, these names illustrate the practice of the wife using the husband's surname (p.40 above) and the practice of using 氏 ('Madam') instead of the wife's own personal name, just mentioned.

Husband	*Wife*	
Lim Meng Chew	Lim Tim Tee	('Lim' - her husband's surname;
林明照	林覃氏	'Tim' - her own surname;
		'Tee' - 'Madam')

Husband	*Wife*
Wong Keng Peng	Wong Tan See
王經變	王陳氏

---

[23] Dyer Ball (1900:400-401) discusses the reluctance of middle-class married women in southern China to reveal their personal names.

A name such as the following (being the name of a young Hainanese woman) can easily lead to confusion:

Fan Yap Lan 龐葉蘭	Both 'Fan' and 'Yap' can be used as surnames, and it might appear that this woman's real surname is 'Yap', and that she is married to a man surnamed 'Fan', whose surname she has put in front of her own; in this case however, it is discovered that her father's surname is 'Fan', and it follows therefore that her own surname must also be 'Fan', and that 'Yap' must be a personal name.

It is important to note that 'shih' *always follows immediately after a woman's own surname (her maiden name).*

Married Women — Use of husbands' surname and own personal name

Married Chinese women who have travelled widely, or have had considerable contact with western customs, will sometimes choose instead to be known after marriage by their husbands' surname and their own personal names just as for example a Miss Mary Stokes who married a man named Brown might be known after marriage as Mrs. Mary Brown. So with the Chinese; if a Hokkien woman named Tan Tiew Choon (陳綢春) marries a man surnamed Khaw she may choose to be known after marriage as Khaw Tiew Choon (許綢春).

43

III The Chinese Characters of Names

Each character represents a separate (monosyllabic) word. Chinese names may be written:

    (a) from left to right; or
    (b) from right to left; or
    (c) from top to bottom

As illustration, a common name Lim Ah Lai may be used. This is written in Chinese: 林 Lim; 亞 Ah; 來 Lai.

The surname, of course, is Lim. This may be written, then, either:

    (a) from left to right -   林亞來
    (b) from right to left -   來亞林
    (c) from top to bottom -   林
                                       亞
                                       來

The name must be read, of course, in the same order as it is written, so that whichever way it is written it will be read in this order - Lim Ah Lai.

The method adopted by the present Government of China is in accordance with (a), that is to write, and print, in horizontal lines from left to right, following the western practice.

Methods of indexing names according to their Chinese characters

There are two fairly common systems in use, depending upon the Chinese character itself, and not on any romanized form of the name. The words in Chinese dictionaries are arranged following the order of one of these two systems.

Indexing by the 'Radical' Method

This system depends upon the 'Radical' (字部 *Mand*.: tzu-pu *Hok*.: ji-po) of the Chinese character. Each Chinese character either includes, or consists of, a radical. The radical often gives a clue to the meaning of the character. Unless the character is itself a radical, it will include a number of additional strokes which are often called the 'phonetic', and which sometimes give an indication of the way the word should be pronounced.

There are in all 214 Chinese radicals, which are arranged and numbered in conventional order; those consisting of one stroke come first, then those consisting of two strokes, and so on down to Radical No. 214, which consists of 17 strokes.[1]

The first four radicals are: 1. 一 2. | 3. 丶 4. 丿

Here are some examples of the way that Chinese words are made up from radicals and phonetics (with Mandarin pronunciation):

Word	Pronounced	Meaning	Radical & Meaning	Phonetic & Pronunciation
丁	Ting	A male adult	一 One	
仲	Chung	2nd of 3 brothers	人 A man	中 Chung
伍	Wu	Five, a squad[2]	人 A man	五 Wu
安	An	Peace	宀 A roof	女 Nu
宋	Sung	To dwell	宀 A roof	木 Mu
明	Ming	Bright	日 Sun	月 Yueh
杜	Tu	To shut out	木 Wood	土 T'u
林	Lin	A forest	木 Wood	木 Mu
柏	Pai	Cedar tree	木 Wood	白 Pai
江	Chiang	A river[3]	水 Water	工 Kung

[1] Newnham (1971, 49:64) remarks on the fact that the actual numbering of radicals is a strictly western procedure — Chinese do not use these numbers for the radicals. He also draws attention to the new Pinyin dictionary using 186 radicals instead of 214.

[2] The radical of a character is sometimes written in a different form when used in combination with other strokes. The radical written here in its normal form 人, in the first column has been modified to 亻 for ease of writing when combined with other strokes. Other examples are given in Appendix C.

46

汪	Wang	Expanse of water	水 Water	王	Wang
陳	Ch'en	To arrange[4]	阜 A mound of earth	東	Tung

Incidentally, any of the words listed in the left-hand column may be used as a surname.

Under this system of indexing, each Chinese word is allocated to whichever group its radical entitles it to belong.

Since some of the groups are large (for example, the group with the 'Water' radical consists of more than four hundred words), the characters within each group are arranged according to the number of strokes needed to write them, (excluding the radical itself), with the characters requiring least strokes coming first.

Indexing by the 'Number of Strokes'

The other popular system for the indexing of Chinese words, (used in such lists as telephone directories) arranges the words according to the total number of strokes used to write them, starting with the words with the least number and going on to those with the greatest number. Thus all words consisting of one stroke will be grouped together, then those consisting of two strokes, and so on, up to the complicated characters which may employ up to thirty or more strokes.

The resultant thirty-odd groups of words into which the language is thus divided are still inconveniently large for indexing purposes. A further breakdown is achieved by arranging the words in each group according to their radicals. This system is therefore a transposition of the first system mentioned: the first system makes use of the radical to determine the group to which a word belongs, then the number of additional strokes needed to write the phonetic section (excluding the radical) to determine its precise position in that group; the second system uses the total

---

[3] When standing alone, this radical is written 水 ; when in combination, however, it is generally written 氵

[4] Here again, the radical which when standing alone is written 阜, takes a modified form, namely 阝 , when in combination.

Figure 3: The number of strokes method of indexing.

A section of the Chinese telephone directory for the Federation of Malaya, July 1957. This shows subscribers in Kuala Lipis, Pahang. The entries are listed according to the number of strokes in the key word; this illustration depicts words with from two to seven strokes – the following entries go up to fifteen strokes. The key word is the left hand character for each row. Most entries are names of businesses, not surnames. The number on the left is the telephone number (Kuala Lipis exchange).

彭 亨 州

立 啤

KUALA LIPIS

二 劃

75 ········· 人海旅店菜館 ··················· 大街八二號

三 劃

95 ········· 大美公司 ··················· 大街八三號

四 劃

49 ········· 公昌(立卑)有限公司 ····· 大街一〇八號
7 ········· 中央旅社 ····· 立卑大街一〇〇號樓上
11 ········· 中華學校 ··················· 煲溪加邦
125 ········· 王可賢 ··················· 日來街三號
72 ········· 王輝福 ··················· 大街一〇六號
66 ········· 王調 ··················· 大街九三號
114 ········· 天國戲院 ··················· 日來街
131 ········· 仁發興脚車商 ··················· 大街八四號

五 劃

97 ········· 立啤合作社有限公司 ········· 大街八九號
112 ········· 立啤俱樂部
84 ········· 半島旅店 ··················· 大街七二號
162 ········· 打耶峇里ＡＨ ··················· 大街八七號

number of strokes to determine which group a word shall belong to, and uses the radical to determine its position in the group.

To illustrate this method, given below is a selection of seven consecutive words chosen from the 'six-strokes' group of a Chinese dictionary; (Nos. 3, 4, 6 & 7 may be used as surnames; the remainder are common words):

Character - Meaning			*Radical - Meaning*	
1.	好 -	Good	- 女	Woman
2.	奸 -	Wicked; selfish	- 女	Woman
3.	如 -	As if; supposing	- 女	Woman
4.	字 -	A Chinese character	- 子	Child
5.	存 -	To exist	- 子	Child
6.	安 -	Peace	- 宀	Roof
7.	宇 -	Universe	- 宀	Roof

This method is often chosen for compiling lists of words for practical use, because even without knowing much Chinese one can soon learn how to calculate roughly the number of strokes in a word. I have used this method in my list of surnames in Appendix E. This "Purcell" system of indexing was used in the Chinese Affairs Department in Singapore from the beginning.[5] It was also used in the Federation of Malaya telephone directories — Figure 3 is taken from a 1957 directory, showing telephone numbers for Kuala Lipis in Pahang. The heading reads "Two strokes". We get only one two-stroke entry, and below it the heading 'Three strokes', again with only one entry. The left hand column shows the telephone number, and the left hand Chinese character in each case is the name (in many cases of a business). Shown also are the four-, five-, six- and seven-stroke entries.

The number of strokes in each of the three characters of a person's name can also be employed to tell his fortune, to indicate whether the coming year will be auspicious or inauspicious. The method is set out in the almanacs.[6]

---

[5] Information from Mr Blythe.

[6] See Palmer, 1993:149; also see Evelyn Lip, 1994:105-110,143-163.

The Chinese Commercial Code (or C.C.C.)

It will be apparent that, before the introduction of the fax, the usual methods of transmission of cables and telegrams in western languages could not suffice for the transmission of Chinese. Whereas western languages employ twenty- or thirty-odd letters of an alphabet for the transcription of a message, Chinese may require any of eight or ten thousand characters, and it obviously would not be feasible to allot separate Morse values direct to such a great number.

The Chinese Commercial Code (C.C.C.), sometimes called the Chinese Telegraphic Code (C.T.C.), or simply Telecode, was devised, with the approval of the Ministry of Communications of the former National Government of China, to overcome this difficulty. Its conception is simple: each character in a Chinese dictionary was allotted a number, the first being enumerated 0001, the second 0002, and so on. When a message in Chinese was to be transmitted, each character was converted into a number; when the string of numbers reached the receiving office, each number was reconverted into a Chinese character, thus giving the message in Chinese written form.

The dictionary selected for this was compiled according to the 'Radical' arragement, the former of the two systems mentioned above. To give an example, the legend: c.c.c. 2651-0068-0046 stands for the characters 林亞九 (Lim Ah Kow in the Hokkien pronunciation).

The original compilation of the Chinese Commercial Code comprised less than 8,000 basic characters. Since then revised editions have been published giving additional characters.

An important step was the introduction of a new enlarged version by the the Chinese People's Government (Ministry of Posts, Telegraph and Telephone) in May 1952, called the Standard Chinese Telegraphic Code (S.T.C.). In this about 650 entries were revised. All the c.c.c. numbers given in these notes are from the earlier unrevised editions of the Code. (To distinguish between the two codes, look up the character for No.0049 - in the older C.C.C. it is 乩 and in the newer S.T.C. it is 乾.)

The number of additional characters varies in the different versions, but of course no version goes beyond 9999 as the code

Figure 4: Chinese Commercial Code (C.C.C.)

This reproduces the first page of the code from an almanac published in Hongkong for year 1991-92. As can be seen from the left edge, this shows only one side of the fold-back page – compare this with Figure 6, which shows both sides, the page being opened out. The heading in the right margin reads 'Tien pao hsin pien' ("New telegraphic list"); the character in 0049 confirms that it is the later version.

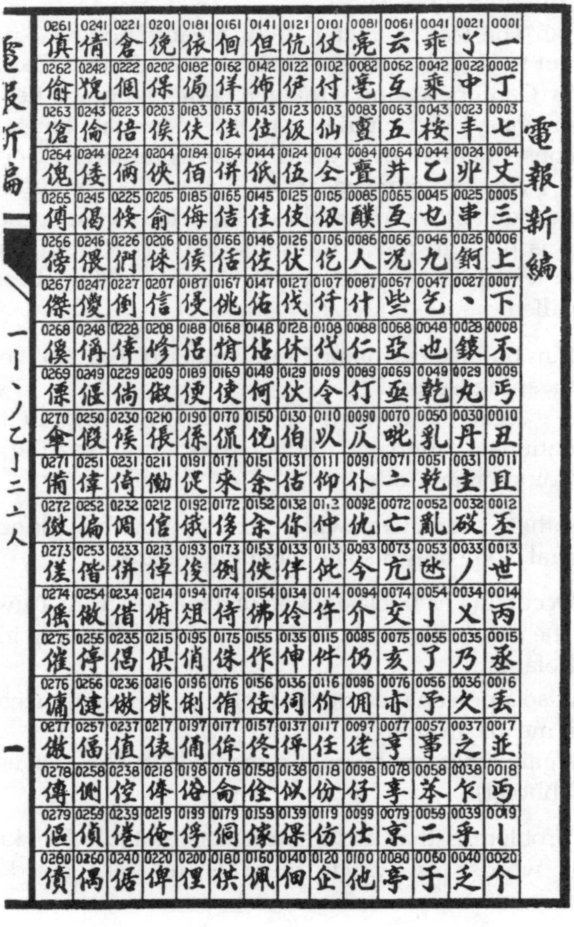

電報新編

0261 傎	0241 倩	0221 倉	0201 俛	0181 依	0161 佪	0141 但	0121 伉	0101 仗	0081 亮	0061 云	0041 乖	0021 丫	0001 一
0262 偷	0242 俔	0222 個	0202 保	0182 偏	0162 佯	0142 佈	0122 伊	0102 付	0082 亳	0062 互	0042 乘	0022 中	0002 丁
0263 傖	0243 倫	0223 倍	0203 俟	0183 佚	0163 佳	0143 位	0123 伋	0103 仙	0083 亶	0063 五	0043 桉	0023 丰	0003 七
0264 傀	0244 倭	0224 倆	0204 俠	0184 佰	0164 併	0144 低	0124 伍	0104 仝	0084 亹	0064 井	0044 乙	0024 丱	0004 丈
0265 傅	0245 偊	0225 倏	0205 俞	0185 侮	0165 佶	0145 住	0125 伎	0105 仅	0085 醮	0065 亙	0045 乜	0025 串	0005 三
0266 傍	0246 偎	0226 們	0206 俫	0186 侯	0166 佸	0146 佐	0126 伏	0106 仡	0086 人	0066 況	0046 九	0026 銅	0006 上
0267 傑	0247 儍	0227 倒	0207 信	0187 侵	0167 佻	0147 佑	0127 伐	0107 仟	0087 什	0067 些	0047 乞	0027 丶	0007 下
0268 傒	0248 倆	0228 倖	0208 修	0188 侶	0168 悄	0148 佔	0128 休	0108 代	0088 仁	0068 亞	0048 也	0028 鑲	0008 不
0269 傈	0249 偓	0229 倘	0209 做	0189 便	0169 使	0149 何	0129 伙	0109 令	0089 仃	0069 亟	0049 乾	0029 丸	0009 丐
0270 傘	0250 假	0230 候	0210 倀	0190 係	0170 侃	0150 侻	0130 伯	0110 以	0090 仄	0070 吡	0050 乳	0030 丹	0010 丑
0271 備	0251 偉	0231 倚	0211 働	0191 促	0171 來	0151 余	0131 估	0111 仰	0091 仆	0071 亠	0051 乾	0031 主	0011 且
0272 儌	0252 偏	0232 倜	0212 倌	0192 俄	0172 侈	0152 佘	0132 你	01,2 仲	0092 仇	0072 亡	0052 亂	0032 破	0012 丕
0273 僕	0253 偕	0233 倂	0213 倬	0193 俊	0173 例	0153 佚	0133 伴	0113 仳	0093 今	0073 亢	0053 迯	0033 丿	0013 世
0274 僊	0254 傲	0234 借	0214 俯	0194 俎	0174 侍	0154 佛	0134 伶	0114 仵	0094 介	0074 交	0054 亅	0034 乂	0014 丙
0275 催	0255 停	0235 偈	0215 俱	0195 俏	0175 侏	0155 作	0135 伸	0115 件	0095 仍	0075 亥	0055 了	0035 乃	0015 丞
0276 傭	0256 健	0236 傚	0216 俳	0196 俐	0176 侑	0156 佞	0136 伺	0116 价	0096 佣	0076 亦	0056 予	0036 久	0016 丟
0277 儆	0257 偪	0237 值	0217 俵	0197 俑	0177 侔	0157 佟	0137 伻	0117 任	0097 佬	0077 亨	0057 事	0037 之	0017 並
0278 傳	0258 側	0238 倥	0218 俸	0198 俗	0178 侖	0158 佺	0138 似	0118 份	0098 仔	0078 享	0058 苶	0038 乍	0018 丏
0279 傴	0259 偵	0239 倦	0219 俺	0199 俘	0179 侗	0159 傢	0139 倮	0119 仿	0099 仕	0079 京	0059 二	0039 乎	0019 丨
0280 債	0260 偶	0240 倨	0220 俾	0200 俚	0180 供	0160 佩	0140 佃	0120 企	0100 他	0080 亭	0060 于	0040 乏	0020 个

電報新編

一丨丶丿乙亅二亠人

一

limits itself to only four digits. Even with the inclusion of the additional words, there are occasional local words occurring in Chinese names which will not be found in the Chinese Commercial Code; for instance, there is a Teochew man whose name is:

彭大冇 Peh Tai Par:

> The first two Chinese characters can be found in the code (numbers 1756-1129).
>
> The last character 冇 (it means 'hollow', 'porous') is not to be found; it is used in the Teochew dialect, and also in Cantonese and Hokkien, but is not to be found in ordinary dictionaries of the national language; and consequently not in the Chinese Commercial Code.
>
> Again, the word (spelt Boh or Boo) is quite common in the names of Hainanese, especially Hainanese women; it is used in much the same way as 亞 (Ah) is used by other Chinese; for example, there is a Hainanese woman called:

林妚二 Lim Boh Jee (surname Lim: Boh used like 'Ah'; Jee meaning 'second')

> Again, the word is not to be found in the usual national language dictionaries, nor in the Chinese Commercial Code.

A few other characters which could not be found in the Commercial Code may also be mentioned here:

溧	Occurring as the last name of a teacher from Taiwan.
畾	The personal name of a Hakka merchant living in Kelantan.
洴	Also a personal name (In Hokkien it is romanized Chia[n], it means 'in sipid').
欉	Again a personal name (romanized in Hokkien as Chhong).

The problem is that in some dialects, notably Hokkien, there are local words for which there is no recognised Chinese character.

Copies of the Chinese Commercial Code can be purchased quite cheaply in Chinese book shops in Malaysia; it is known in Chinese as:

明密碼　*Mand.*: Ming Mi Ma (The Hokkien name is Kng Am Be),
　　or
電報新編 *Mand.*: Tien pao hsin pien (*Hok.*: Tien po sin pien).

It is also reproduced in most of the Chinese almanacs (similar to the English Old Moore's Almanac) which are on sale in sundry shops at the turn of the Chinese year. The codes in these almanacs are discussed by Palmer[7], under the heading "Telegram Numeration of Chinese Characters". The older codes used Chinese digits for the numbers, but nowadays western digits are used, as shown in Figure 4; this reproduces the first page of such a list found in an almanac for the year 1991-2 published in Hong Kong.

There is a similar compilation, though for some reason less used,[8] whereby three letters are used to represent each Chinese character, instead of the four-digit number just mentioned. The examples below (the first five characters of the code) illustrate this:

Chinese character	c.c.c. number	c.c.c. letter
一	0001	AAB
丁	0002	AAC
七	0003	AAD
丈	0004	AAE
三	0005	AAF

Some lists give both the four digits and the three letters for each character.

For communications purposes, the Chinese commercial code has been made almost redundant by the introduction of the fax

---

[7] 1993:152-3.

[8] Mr Blythe offers the explanation that Chinese find no difficulty in handling the codes with the four-digit numbers, since the numbers are familiar to them (particularly the codes which employ the Chinese digits), while the letters of a western alphabet are of course strange to many Chinese.

and the internet: Chinese characters can now be transmitted directly in pictorial form as they are written. But the code has proved valuable in other ways, notably as a means for the recording and handling of Chinese names by people who do not read Chinese characters. Its advantage is that each number represents one definite Chinese character precisely and unambiguously, unlike romanized spellings which appear in differing forms, vary according to the dialect being represented, and often do not indicate the tone of the word.[9] This quality makes it invaluable for librarians for instance, although I do not know of its being widely used in that field. It certainly has been exploited by police and security authorities, including the U.S. Central Intelligence Agency, who have consequently produced some good editions of the code. The only necessity is that at the outset a person proficient in Chinese is needed to find the correct Chinese commercial code number for a given character.[10] Thereafter, the four-digit number is to all intents and purposes the same as the character, and can be used in recording and transmitting it.

The Giles System
In preference to the Chinese Commercial Code some foreigners (but few Chinese) make use of the Giles numbers. In 1892, H.A. Giles, one-time British Consul at Ningpo, published a Chinese-English dictionary in which each Chinese word is listed alphabetically according to its spelling in the national language; the words are numbered serially from beginning to end thus:

A 阿 is number 1, A 啊 is number 2, A 腌 is number 3 and so on through the alphabet to Yün 薀 which is number 13,848.

---

[9] "The written characters, not the spoken words, are consistently in one form, and are therefore the stable representations of names despite all individual and regional dialect versions" (C.I.A. 1961:1).

[10] Where a romanized spelling of the name is available as well as the character, even someone who is not proficient in written Chinese can ascertain the c.c.c. number by using an appropriate index; I do not know whether such indexes are available generally.

54

Non-Chinese would find it easy to ascertain the Giles numbers, since the words are arranged alphabetically. But with the Giles system a character may be represented by a number which may have from one to five digits, making it less attractive to use than the more foolproof four-digit numbers used in the Chinese Commercial Code.

Transcription of Chinese names back into Chinese

From time to time Chinese newspapers translate into Chinese, and publish, items of news appearing in English (or other foreign-language), newspapers; if the report mentions Chinese names in romanized form, it is difficult for the translators to ascertain the correct Chinese characters which those names represent, since one spelling in English can often represent several different Chinese words. In such a contingency, the Chinese translation will give what it believes to be the correct characters for the name, but in order to show that it is a transcription, and not necessarily the correct character, adds the following words:

譯音 (*Mand.*: i yin; *Hok.*: ek im)   'Translation-sound', i.e. Transcription.

For example, a scholar whose name is 洪智慧 (Ang Tee Hwee) is mentioned in a news report in an English newspaper. The spelling 'Ang Tee Hwee' could represent any of several characters in Chinese; a Chinese newspaper reproducing the report guesses that the correct characters must be 汪知非 and prints accordingly:

汪知非譯音 ('Ang Tee Hwee as transcribed')

Although this name is similarly pronounced Ang Tee Hwee in English, it will be seen that the Chinese characters are not identical with the correct name.[11]

Abbreviations of Chinese characters

As with other languages, a number of Chinese words can be written in short forms, and these forms are commonly used for

---

[11] Nio Joe Lan (1933:416) describes the same practice in the Netherlands Indies press.

writing people's names. These short forms can be very confusing to the uninitiated, and complicate the search for characters in Chinese dictionaries.

In the short form, the radical of the character generally remains unchanged, the phonetic part being reduced to a simpler form. Here are a few examples of recognised abbreviations:

Character	c.c.c. no.	Radical	Abbreviation
僂	(0283)	亻	偻
勵	(0536)	力	励
檳	(2919)	木	槟

In the following, however, the radical itself has been omitted altogether:

凰	(0420)	几	皇
復	(1788)	彳	复
雲	(7189)	雨	云

It sometimes happens that the short form of a word is identical with the normal written character for a different word; some examples of this:

Character	Abbreviation	Mandarin	Identical Character	Mandarin
伙	(0129)	火	huo (utensils)	火	huo (fire)
潘	(3476)	沈	shen (to leak)	沈	ch'en (to sink, perish)

When this occurs, only the context will indicate in which sense the character is to be read. It goes without saying that the pronunciation and meaning of a word are not affected when it is written in the short form. Lists of the accepted abbreviations for common characters are widely published, and they are now commonly used in the standard Chinese dictionaries.

Homonyms — which surname is meant?

When we see a Chinese surname written down, we can be reasonably certain that we know which surname it is. But if it is spoken, particularly in a plural society like Malaysia where several Chinese dialects are in use, it may not be clear which name is meant, since several different surnames may have a similar pronunciation.

An obvious solution is to write the character, (if there is no paper handy, it is often written with one finger in the air, or on a convenient surface like the windscreen of a car). But many of these "homogenous" surnames can be identified more readily with a verbal description.

Giles[12] describes how, in China, features of a particular Chinese character were used to distinguish it from other characters. For example (retaining his Mandarin spelling), the surname 張 Chang (C1728, Teoh in Hokkien) would be described as 弓長張 'Kung-ch'ang Chang"; and 李 Li (C2621, Lee in Hokkien) would be 木子李 or 'Mu-tzû Li'; one can see how the character is identified by mentioning its components separately.

Also 林 Lin (C2651, Lim in Hokkien) can be called (in Hokkien) 'Nng bok e Lim' "Two trees Lim". 陳 Ch'ên (C7115 Hok. Tan) is called 耳東陳 'Êrh-tung Ch'ên' "Ear east Ch'ên'; in Penang I have heard (Amoy) 'Hï-á pêng Tân' "Ear-side Tân" used.

王 Wang (C3769, Ong in Hokkien) would be 三畫王 'San-hua Wang' ("Three-strokes Wang"); I have heard this description used in Malaysia also.

Finally, also from Giles is 黄 Huang (C7806, Ng or Ooi in Hokkien), giving 草頭黄 'Ts'ao-t'ou Huang' ("Grass-head Huang"); it is sometimes known less elegantly in Malaysia as (Hok.) 'Toa pak-to e Ooi' "Big-belly Ooi".[13]

Nio Joe Lan[14] records that in the Netherlands Indies the distinguishing of personal names from each other is achieved in the same manner.

---

[12] Giles p 1356; cf. G.M.H. Playfair, 1886. The Colloquial Analysis of Chinese Surnames. *China Branch of the Royal Asiatic Society*. Vol.21, pp.224-6; see also Hauer, 1927:82-5.

[13] Creamer (1995:912) gives other examples. Weig, 1931:3-100 gives the 'distinguishing formula' for many of the surnames in his list, in Chinese and German.

[14] Nio Joe Lan (1933:415).

Erroneously recording the Chinese characters of names
Those of the Chinese in Malaysia who are not literate in Chinese must rely upon a petition-writer, or educated friend, to write their letters, and to fill in official forms. It is often necessary to include in the letter or form the Chinese characters of the name of the originator, or of some other person mentioned in it. Some people do not know the characters of even their own names, much less those of other persons whom they may mention. Taking the line of least resistance, the person writing the letter will often write the Chinese characters of a name which could represent the name mentioned, although they may be incorrect. For example, a petition mentions a man

    吳仲森   (C 0702-0112-2773) - pronounced in Cantonese
                        Ng Chong Sam.

Another person, not knowing the correct characters, later wrote the name:

    吳鐘桑   (C0702-6988-9753) - pronounced in
                        Cantonese Ng Chong San, and employing
                        incorrect characters for both the personal names.

Another example, this time concerning a Cantonese woman:

Her name is spelt in English: Chan Ah Ho; when she applied for a document at a government office, her name was given in Chinese characters as:

    陳亞好   (C7115-0068-1170) pronounced Chan Ah Ho.
                        To support her application, she produced a letter
                        which had been sent to her from China, on which
                        her correct name was shown as:

    陳翠荷   (C7115-5050-5440) pronounced in Cantonese
                        Chan Chooi Ho. It is an example of the
                        substitution of the word 'Ah' for the first personal
                        name, and of the use of an incorrect character for
                        the second personal name, (although the western
                        spelling of the latter is not affected).

Such examples of names changing, or names being represented by incorrect characters, are very common.

Recognising names in Chinese texts
Since the vast majority of Chinese names (whether surnames or personal names) also exist as ordinary words in their own right, it is sometimes a puzzle to pick out in a document which characters actually denote proper names. To help identify the names, writers sometimes underline the characters referring to personal or place names; if the text is written vertically, side-lining is used instead[15].

Numbers used in names: The Chinese characters.
Generally numbers occurring in names (mentioned above, p.25) are written in the Chinese figures 一, 二, 三, etc., but sometimes longer forms are used instead. These long forms correspond to the western numbers 'One', 'Two', 'Three', etc., and are used in the writing of accounts to prevent fraud. Since a name may be written sometimes with the short form and sometimes with the long form, the alternative forms for the first five numbers given below will be found useful for reference.

Short form	1	2	3	4	5
(c.c.c)	0001	0059	0005	0934	0063
	一	二	三	四	五
Long form	One	Two	Three	Four	Five
(c.c.c)	1105	1708	0638	5127	0124
	壹	式	叁	肆	伍

(But it is more usual for the first-born to be given the name 大 Ta (c.c.c. 1129) meaning 'great' than one of the names for 'One' given here).

For example, a Cantonese woman writes her name in Chinese:

Chinese	*Cantonese spelling*	*In English*
哀二女 (sic)	Yuen Yee Moy	surname-'two'-'woman'
(5913-0059-1166)		

---

[15] Creamer, 1995:911-2.

But a letter sent to her from China is addressed to:

哀式女
(5913-1708-1166)　The Cantonese spelling and meaning in English
remain unchanged, although the alternative
form of writing the middle character ('two') has
been used.

IV Western Spelling (Romanization) of Chinese Names

While western writing is phonetic, Chinese characters are ideographic; that is to say, each character represents an idea, rather than a sound.[1] In this respect Chinese characters may be compared with the numerals used in the West. For example, the numeral '4' represents the same idea to any European, regardless of the language he speaks. However, this numeral will not be read with the same sound by people who speak the various languages current in Europe. In English it will be read 'Four', in German 'Vier', in French 'Quatre' and so on.

One of the commonest Chinese surnames is written 王. This character will suggest to all literate Chinese the idea of 'King' or 'Royal', but its pronunciation will vary according to the native dialect of the speaker. In the national language (Mandarin) it is pronounced 'Wang'; in Cantonese 'Wong'; in Teochew 'Heng', and so on.

Although attempts have been made at various times to standardize the romanization of Chinese words, it will usually be found in Malaysia that the romanized spelling of Chinese names varies according to the native dialect of the person referred to, and to the native dialect and personal preference of the writer.[2] Consequently, the transcription of a name in even one dialect may take one of several forms. To take an extreme example, the word

---

[1] This image is an over-simplification, but will serve our purposes here; for the persuasive argument that Chinese characters represent words rather than ideas, see for example Boltz, 1994:3-9.

[2] Nio Joe Lan (1933:412) writes (in Dutch) "Of course every bearer of a name has the right, insofar as it depends on him, to romanize his name in whatever way he chooses, in accordance with the dialect he uses".

61

郭 (C6753) may be transcribed in the Hokkien dialect alone as either Keh, or Koay, or Koeh, or Kwek, or Quay, or Queh, or Quek, or Koid, or Koek, or Keah or Keak.

It will be seen, therefore, that a given Chinese name can be spelt in several different ways in Roman script; and conversely a romanized name can sometimes represent several different Chinese characters.

It sometimes happens that a person's surname may be romanized in one dialect, and his given name in another dialect; for example, there is a man with the name 陳才 who spells his name Tan Choy; Tan is the Hokkien pronunciation of the first character, and Choy is the Cantonese pronunciation of the second character.

Here is an example of a Chinese name, giving the spelling in the different dialects:

Chinese	Mandarin	Hokkien	Cantonese	Hakka	Hainanese	Teochew
張	Chang	Teoh	Cheong	Chong	Chiang	Teo
水	Shui	Swee	Sui	Sooi	Chooi	Chooi

It will be seen that the pronunciations in the different dialects do bear some resemblance to each other. [This is an example of a name which consists of a surname and *one* personal name only (See p.20, above). It is also an illustration of the use of one of the five elements (水 – water) as a given name (p.22 above).

What at first sight appear to be deviant or variant spellings for a particular dialect may turn out to be due to differences of subdialect. For example in the list in Appendix B, No.7806, for the Hokkien spelling we find both 'Ooi' and 'Ng'. Both spellings are commonly found in Malaysia. The first is a satisfactory spelling for the Chiangchew subdialect, the second is equally satisfactory for Amoy and other subdialects of Hokkien.[3] Many other examples could be cited.

---

[3] See Tan Pow Tek, 1924:60. He refers to the Chiangchew as the *Ch'it Kuan* ('seven districts') pronunciation, and the other as the *Goh Kuan* ('five districts') pronunciation. On these terms see, e.g. Pitcher, 1912:10 (under 'Chang-chow' and Chuan-chow'); or Franke & Chen, 1, 1982:49, Nos.3 & 4.

Some equivalent English, French and Dutch spellings for surnames
The position is complicated by the differing spelling systems used
by non-Chinese for the romanization of Chinese names. The
following table illustrates some of the differences between
common English, French and Dutch spellings. It is taken from an
article written in Dutch to guide librarians, and no Chinese
characters are given.[4]

English	French	Dutch
Chang	Tchang	Tsjang
Chao	Tchao	Tsjao
Chên	Tchen	Tsjenn
Chêng	Tcheng	Tsjeng
Chu	Tchou	Tsjoe
Fu	Fou	Foe
Hsü	Hiu	Hsu
Hu	Hou	Hoe
Huang	Hoang	Hwang
Hung	Hong	Hoeng
Ku	Kou	Koe
Kuo	Kouo	Kwo
Liu	Lieou	Lioe
Lo	Louo	Lwo
Mu	Mou	Moe
Shên	Chen	Sjenn
Shih	Che	Sje
Shu	Chou	Sjoe
Su	Sou	Soe
Wu	Ou	Woe

Note
In China formerly the newspapers used the English romanization
for names; the Catholic Church tended to use the French
romanization.[5]

---

[4] Thys, E., 1952. Enkele "Tips" voor de Transcriptie van Chinese Eigennamen. *Bibkliotheekkunde* **23** (Antwerp) 3-12. I thank Drs René Teygeler for supplying a copy of this article to me.

[5] Weig, 1931:ix.

The Indonesian spelling of Chinese names

It is not surprising — in view of the former Netherlands influence there — that the spelling of Chinese names in Indonesia has followed the Dutch orthography. Given below are examples of the more common differences of spelling between the Dutch style romanization in Indonesia and the English style romanization in Malaysia:

Conventional spelling in Malaysia	Conventional spelling in Indonesia	Examples (Malaysian)	Examples (Indonesian)
Ah	A	Lee Ah Yau	Lie A Yau
Ay	E	Say	Se
Ch	Tj or Tjh	Chin	Tjin or Tjhin
-ck	-k	Teck	Tek
E	I	Leong; Teoh	Liong; Tio
Ee	Ie	Tee; Bee	Tie; Bie
I	Ie	Lim; Sim	Liem; Siem
Iew	Ioe	Siew	Sioe
J	Dj	Jim; Jee	Djim; Djie
Oo	Oe	Choo	Tjoe
Ooi	Oei	Ooi	Oei
U	Oe	Lui; Siu	Loei; Sioe
-u	-uw	Liau	Liauw
Wee	Oei or Oey	Wee; Swee	Oei; Soey
Y	J	Yap; Yek	Jap; Jek

Some Chinese names spelt in the Indonesian Manner

Indonesian spelling	Chinese	Chinese Commercial Code Numbers	What the equivalent Malaysian spelling would be (The sex is also shown)
Gan Soey Tjeng	顔瑞清	7346-3843-3237	Gan Swee Cheng (M)
Go See Tjong	吳世璋	0702-0013-3864	Goh Say Chong (M)
Hie Tjoe Kim	許珠金	6079-3796-6855	Hee Choo Kim (F)
Ho Foe Wong	何富旺	0149-1381-2489	Ho Foo Wong (M)
Jap Kie Hai	葉矩海	5509-4251-3189	Yap Koo Hai (M)
Joe Se Djoe	尤四裕	1429-6007-5940	Yew Say Joo (M)
Khoe Sioe Kim	丘秀琴	8003-4423-3830	Khoo Siew Kim (F)
Liauw A Njan	廖亞元	1675-0068-0337	Liau Ah Nyan (M)
Lie Bie Tjie	李美濟	2621-5019-3444	Lee Bee Chee (M)
Liem Heng Hwat	林弘發	2651-1738-4099	Lim Heng Huat (M)
Lim Po Tjoe	林寶珠	2651-1405-3796	Lim Po Choo (M)

Lim Tjie Tjhoi	林志楚	2651-1805-2806	Lim Chee Chho (M)
Ng A Loei	伍亞女	0124-0068-1166	Ng Ah Looi (F)
Ng Giok Tjin	黄玉珍	7806-3768-3791	Ng Geok Chin (F)
Njo Soei Liong	梁瑞隆	2733-3843-7127	Neoh Swee Leong (M)
Oei Gwan Swie	黄源瑞	7806-3293-3843	Ooi Guan Swee (M)
Oen Jin Tjoi	溫仁才	3306-0088-2088	Oon Yin Choy (M)
Sie Loe Eng	薛裕英	5641-5940-5391	See Loo Eng (M)
Tan Ho Sioe	陳和瑞	7115-0735-3843	Tan Hoe Swee
Tio Tjoe Liang	張珠良	1728-3796-5328	Teoh Choo Liang (M)
Tjan Tek Tjoh	陳德初	7115-1795-0443	Chan Teck Choh (M)
Tjong Tui Oe	鍾對宇	6945-1417-1342	Choong Tooi Oo (M)
Wong Sai Tjan	黄細珍	7806-4798-3791	Wong Sei Chan (M)
Yap A Tjoen	葉亞轉	5509-0068-6567	Yap Ah Choon (F)

Nio Joe Lan draws attention to a further complication regarding Chinese names in the 1930s in the Netherlands Indies. The Netherlands Indies press transcribed the names of Chinese residents of the Indies in the Dutch spelling as shown here, according to the Hokkien or other local dialect. But the names of prominent persons in China were rendered in the (English) Wade-Giles system, and of course according to the Mandarin pronunciation. This in spite of the fact that in the Dutch press in Holland itself the names of Chinese leaders in China were spelt after the Dutch fashion, so that Chiang Kai Shek's name appeared as Tsjiang Kai Sjek.[6]

The Chinese in Indonesia adopt Indonesian names

One of the striking features that emerges from our study of Chinese naming customs is the persistence with which a core of the Chinese in the Nanyang have clung to their age-old traditions. It is salutary to look at the experience of the Chinese residents of neighbouring Indonesia, and to be forced to modify our view profoundly. One consequence of Indonesian independence gained in the 1940s has been the gradual but relentless suppression of manifestations of Chinese culture. By the 1990s this is virtually complete. The Chinese there no longer display Chinese characters for shop-signs or other purposes; no processions will be seen marking Chinese New Year, or for weddings or funerals; the

---

[6] Nio Joe Lan, 1933:413.

Chinese language schools have been closed; for nearly everyone except the elderly, the Chinese dialects have given way to Bahasa Indonesia.

In conformity with this trend towards assimilation with Indonesian culture, nearly all Indonesian Chinese now use Indonesian names, having changed even their Chinese surnames. The name-changing process was given a boost by a decree of President Suharto dated 27 December 1966,[7] which simplified the procedure of an earlier Ordinance.[8] The declared aim of the decree was to accelerate the assimilation of Indonesian citizens of foreign descent into the body of the Indonesian nation; it encouraged the adoption of Indonesian names by Indonesians of foreign descent and specifically provided for Indonesian citizens still using Chinese names to be given full facilities to change their names to ordinary Indonesian names. The name-changing procedure was so simplified that Chinese could notify their intention to adopt Indonesian names to the local district office, and as soon as they had done so, could thereupon start using the new name officially. At the end of three months, provided there was no objection, the new name was regarded as officially confirmed. This procedure, which was intended to be of limited duration, came into effect on 1 January 1967.

In a later decree by President Suharto, in 1967,[9] the Indonesian Government reiterated its desire that Indonesian citizens of foreign descent who still used Chinese names should adopt Indonesian names; but it seems that it was only the Chinese with Indonesian citizenship who were expected to take Indonesian names.

The procedure for applying for a change of name in Indonesia is set out in Wirjono Alisardjono.[10] This book (pp.47-50) also offers suggestions on the choice of Indonesian names by Chinese who wish to "go Indonesian". The suggested examples are

---

[7] No.127/U/Kep/12/1966.

[8] No.4 of 1961.

[9] Issued on 6 December 1967.

[10] *Nama-nama Putra-Putri, Perusahaan dan Toko*. Ekasarana (no date, no place) p.65.

interesting: those with the surname 'Han' could adopt the Indonesian names Handoyo, Handono or Hanjana. For surname 'Oei' it suggests Wiyono, Wiryono, Wijoyo, Wicaksono or Wibisana. Since the writer's own name is Wiryono, we can deduce that he is a Chinese who formerly had the surname 'Oei'. Other examples of adopted Indonesian names (taken from newspaper announcements,) are Tan Liang Soey who took the name Leon Simon Tandijaya; Jo Eng Tjoen, who became Josef E. Trisna Saputra; and Oey Ay Mee who became Regina A. Emmy Wijayanti. (I have adapted the spellings of these Indonesian names to the 1972 EYD system.)

"A frequent answer to the problem of what name to choose has involved splendid renderings of Javanese and Sanskrit titles which at times are so spectacular that they give the game away in advance." For example, Tang Liang Li changed his name to Tubagus Pranata Tirtawidjaya. As would be expected, some have incorporated their Chinese surnames into their new Indonesian names, such as Lim in Salim; Goh in Gozali; Tan in Tanzil; San in Santoso; and Oei in Wijaya. The changing of names has had some bizarre results. It is reported that when waiting at airports Chinese have been known to miss their plane because they did not recognize their own names being called out over the loudspeakers. Also that in the early 1970s, after the Chinese had been encouraged to take Indonesian names, the authorities had some difficulty in the enforcement of unofficial measures to curtail the opportunities open to Chinese, since the Chinese could not always be easily recognized as such. Some faculties in the University of Indonesia "got around the problem by having applicants name their grandparents as well as their parents." This would of course reveal their Chinese origin.[11]

The question as to whether the Chinese in Indonesia adopted Indonesian names voluntarily, or under compulsion, has been much debated. In 1971 even Mr Lee Kuan Yew (Prime Minister of Singapore) entered the public discussion with the assertion that

---

[11] The information in this paragraph is taken from Hugh & Ping-ching Mabbett, 1972. The Chinese Community in Indonesia. In *The Chinese in Indonesia, the Philippines and Malaysia*, pp.3-15. London: The Minority Rights Group.

the Chinese were being forced to adopt Indonesian names. There would seem to be no simple answer.

It will be found that some of the names adopted are of Arabic origin, with decided Muslim associations: Salim, Gozali and Tanzil have been mentioned; to these could be added further examples, such as Arief Husni, Sofyan, Hassan, Hanafi, Suleiman, and Mukmin Ali. I have not seen any indication that those who choose such names are in fact Muslims.

Apart from this, Chinese who are converted to Islam in Indonesia normally take Muslim names in the usual way (see p.38 above). For example a woman named The Giok Sin from Menado became a Muslim in 1965 and is now well-known as Ibu Qomariah.[12]

The Chinese living in Thailand

Family names were introduced into Thai law in 1913 by King Rama VI .[13] Thai surnames (like surnames in the west) are written after the personal name. Accordingly, Chinese who have resided in Thailand for some time generally write their names with the surname after the personal names. Thus a man whose name is Lim Cheng Sim would write his name:

Cheng Sim sae Lim   ('sae' is the transliteration of the Thai
                     word แซ่ which in turn is the Thai
                     transliteration of the Chinese word
                     姓 ('seh') meaning Surname).

Where appropriate the Thai equivalent of 'Mister' will be used before Chinese names as before Thai names; it is 'Nai', written นาย in Thai; thus the name Mr. Lim Cheng Sim written in the Thai way would become:

Nai Cheng Sim sae Lim   ('Mr' Cheng Sim 'surnamed' Lim)

When such names are being written in Chinese script, the character used to represent 'Nai' is 乃 (pronounced Nai, C.C.C.

---

[12] See note by Dr Claudine Salmon in *Archipel*, 25, 1983, p.236.

[13] J.H.C.S. Davidson (ed.) 1987. *Lai Su' Thai, Essays in honour of E.H.S. Simmonds.* University of London. p.42.

68

number 0035, grammatically a conjunctive particle). To give two examples, a Chinese whose personal names are 金邱 Kim Khoo would write his name in Chinese, with the Chinese equivalent of 'Nai' thus:

乃金邱   (Nai Kim Khoo);

and a person whose name was 聰 Thong only would write it:

乃聰   (Nai Thong)

It is important to note that the word 乃 Nai cannot be a Chinese surname, and that the names which immediately follow it will not be the Chinese surname but the personal names; on occasion of course, as in the case of Nai Cheng Sim sae Lim given above, the surname may be appended, but it will be preceded by the word 'sae'.

The Thai equivalent for 'Mrs' is นาง (pronounced 'Nang'), and the translation of 'Miss' is นางสาว (pronounced 'Nangsao'); they are used similarly, for example - Nang Yi Nam sae Tan (i.e. 'Mrs.' Yi Nam 'surnamed' Tan). Further examples of the names of the Chinese people resident in Thailand are given below. They have been arranged alphabetically, according to the spelling used for the surname; the surname in the Thai form, and also that in the form in which a Chinese outside Thailand would normally write it, has been printed in italics to distinguish it from the other names. (I have omitted the titles 'Nai', 'Nang' and 'Nangsao' which occurred in front of some of these names).

Chinese name as used in Thailand	Chinese name as it would be written conventionally	
Kim Sia sae *Ung* (a man, dialect not known)	*Ang* Kim Sia	洪錦城
Yong Chua sae *Chung*	*Chung* Yong Chua	莊英泉
Chianghiang sae *Kao* (a Hokkien woman)	*Khor* Chiang Hiang	許泉香
Tek sae *Khong* (believed to be a man)	*Khong* Tek	孔德

Kimloon sae *Tan* (man, dialect not known)	*Tan* Kim Loon	陳金倫
Oh sae *Tang* (probably Teochew)	*Tang* Oh	陳湖
Ang sae *Tiew* (a Teochew man)	*Teoh* Aun	張紅
Tamfoot sae *Yub*	*Yap* Tam Foot	葉譚佛
Teo sae *Tae* (a man, dialect unknown)	*Teh* Teo*	鄭場

*This man was seen to write his name in Chinese characters:

場姓鄭　　(Teo Seh Teh) following the Thai order.

After longer residence in Thailand, and as they become more identified with the country, Chinese go further, and adopt names which more closely resemble the names of the Thai people themselves; in order to preserve some connection with the all-important surname, they may use it as the basis for the new name, adding on syllables to build up the new name; but in other cases the new surname selected has no discernable similarly with the original Chinese surname.

The list of names below includes examples of Thai names which have an obvious resemblance to the Chinese names, and of those which do not.

Adopted Thai Name	*Chinese name as it would be written conventionally*	
Yongyudth *Chiranakorn* (a Hakka man)	*Cheah* Teh Yoon	謝德潤
Lanfung *Pusat* (a Hainanese woman)	*Foo* Lan Foon	符蘭芬
Saimoei *Kovitaya* (a Hokkien woman)	*Goh* Sai Mei	吳賽梅
Ku Ingek *Kao Ian* (a woman, dialect not given)	*Khaw* Kooi Gaik	許桂玉

M. Sang *Saigham* ('M' for 'monsieur')	*Liong* Tiong Seng	梁長城
Nai Chow Wong *Ratana* ('Nai' for 'mister')	*Low* Haw Cheng	not known
Nai Varin *Chudtharatana* (a man, dialect not known)	*Tan* Chin Hua	陳振華
Prapas *Poonsawasdi*** (a Hokkien man)	*Teoh* Ewe Chong	張有宗

(*This man was born in Thailand; when asked, he said that he had no special reason for choosing this particular Thai name, which does not have any apparent similarity to his Chinese name).

The Chinese living in the Philippines

The Chinese living in the Philippines conform to the normal system of Chinese names, putting the surname first, for example Chua Niu San, Ang Hui Lan, Tan Siu Eng. However, as in Indonesia, the romanized spelling of some names is different from that used in Singapore or Malaysia. For example the common name Wee (the Chiangchew pronunciation of 黄) would be spelt Uy; so we find a name such as Uy Eng Chong. Christian names are popular, so that we find examples of the Chinese surname being used with a Christian name, such as Emelia Uy, Jose Ang; or (a prominent Chinese) Antonio Roxas Chua; or with the whole Chinese name, e.g. Rizal Yuyitung.

As Chinben See observes in the course of a study of the clan system, in the Philippines "assimilated Chinese still keep their distinctive surnames"; in this important respect then they differ from the Chinese in Indonesia and Thailand[14].

---

[14] Chinben See. Chinese Clanship in the Philippine Setting (JSEAS, 12 no.1, 1981, pp.224-247).

V   The Changing of Names

The Changing of surnames

It has been remarked already that Chinese are more jealous of their surnames than are people of the West. It is therefore only with great reluctance that a Chinese will abandon his surname and assume another.

If a person (for example, a fugitive from justice) has a very pressing need to hide his identity by changing his name, he will sometimes change his surname only sufficiently to meet his immediate needs. For example, suppose that a person has the surname 歐 (in Hokkien: Au); if he is obliged to change it, he may merely drop one part of the Chinese character for the name, and call himself 區 which in Hokkien is also pronounced Au, although it is in fact a different surname from that which he had originally[1].

Another of the rare occasions which may justify the changing of a surname is that of the adoption of a child, when as a rule of the child's original surname is dropped, and it is given the surname of the foster father; in fact, it may be said that one of the most compelling reasons for the adoption of a child is in order to perpetuate the family name.[2] A report on Chinese Law and Custom published in Hongkong in 1952 (page 199) reproduces a translation of a deed of the sale of a son for adoption by a Chinese family; the deed includes these words: "Hereafter the vendors

---

[1] For other examples of changing names, see Kiang Kang-hu,1934:131-3.

[2] De Groot makes the point that, in the event of a son and heir dying without issue, if possible the family will adopt a boy who already has the same family name, preferably a near relative. Thus the ancestral tablets will continue in safe hands. It would then be only as a last resort that they would choose a boy with a different family name. De Groot, 1885:91.

cannot go back on their word, or redeem the boy, who is forever prevented from taking back his own father's surname". Another typical provision included in Chinese deeds of adoption, (in this case made in Malaya in 1948), is: " ... I further agree that after the adoption he can bring him up and change his name and surname as he chooses ...".

The surname is changed also in cases of nominal adoption in accordance with the Chinese custom known as 乾親 (*Mand*. Kan Ch'in); I am indebted to Doré for the following quotation:

"When fear is entertained that a child may die, he is adopted into another family, and takes its name. Such adoption is purely nominal. It is not guaranteed by a contract and gives no right to an inheritance. The custom is based on the superstitious notion, that an unlucky lot has befallen the family, and that the only means of preserving a child, is to pass him over fictitiously to a more fortunate household"[3].

Sometimes an adopted child, (especially if it is the son or daughter of a sister, daughter or other female relative), will continue to use its original surname as well as the adoptive surname;[4] for example, suppose that a girl name Khoo Cheng Suan is adopted into a family surnamed Tan; she could thereafter be known as Tan Cheng Suan (i.e. dropping the use of Khoo in favour of Tan). However, so long as her natural parents are alive she may, as a mark of respect to them, continue to use her own family name, preceded by her adoptive surname:

Tan Khoo Cheng Suan.[5]

No doubt she would drop the use of Khoo in due course, but on the occasion of her marriage she would most probably again use both surnames, to let people know that, although she is known by the surname Tan, she originates from the family of Khoo.

---

[3] Henry Doré, 1914. *Researches into Chinese Superstitions*. Shanghai: T'usewei Printing Press, 1, p.23.

[4] Tan Pow Tek (1924:69) states that this would only occur where there "is a strong previous adoption agreement" that the boy retain his original surname.

[5] On this practice, see Kiang Kang-hu, 1934:133.

It may happen that after being adopted into another family, the sickly child recovers. He may then return to his original family, and resume his original surname. For example, a child surnamed Yeap (葉) born in Hokkien province in 1924 was ill constantly, and as a result was handed over to a family surnamed Kow (高) to be brought up. He said later "When I went to live with him I took a new name. I lived in his house for seven years, then when I was well I went back to my parents' house. When I returned to my parents' house I resumed my original name."

But if the adopted son grows up in his adoptive family and has children, the children generally will take his adoptive surname, which is the surname he habitually uses. But it may happen that his natural father and adoptive father may have come to an agreement at the time of his adoption, under which they will have made provision for some of his children to take his original natural surname.

It is interesting to note that in the former Netherlands Indies, a statute promulgated in 1917 laid down very strict conditions for adoption of a boy by a man who had no male offspring.[6]

There is also a rather rare custom amongst Hokkiens, whereby a bridegroom changes his surname on marriage to that of his father-in-law. This custom is called 賣大燈 (In Hokkien Boe Toa Teng), or 'Selling the large lantern', because the marriage ceremony dispenses with the pair of large lanterns which figure prominently at normal Chinese weddings, and upon which the surname of the bridegroom is inscribed.[7]

Freedman even suggests that such bridegrooms "may be considered as male brides", and the husband becomes "a sort of male daughter-in-law", for he "goes out to beget children who will take the surname of his father-in-law".[8] Certainly this kind of marriage is arranged usually by a person who has daughters but

---

[6] De Bruin, 1918:115 (The reference was Stbl. 129 of 1 October 1917, Arts. 5-15).

[7] On this custom, see p.126. Cobbold (1988:209) carries a drawing of two large lanterns in a marriage procession. A French visitor to China wrote, in 1754, that the lanterns were survivals of former times when weddings took place at night (*Inde, Chine et Japon . . .* , Paris: Lehuby, p.211).

[8] Freedman, 1957:122-3.

no sons, and who therefore invites his son-in-law to take the place of a son. Chinese regard for surnames is such that a prospective son-in-law will not consent to this arrangement unless he stands to gain substantially by the marriage. On the other hand, as T'ien Ju-k'ang points out, the son-in-law does become a full member of his father-in-law's clan.[9]

Tan Chee-beng writes that such matrilocal marriages "were not common in Southeast China, as they were rather degrading to the male ... In the Straits Settlements (i.e. Melaka, Singapore and Penang), however, matrilocal marriage was commonly practised in the nineteenth and early twentieth centuries ... ".[10]

There are variations of this custom common in Malaysia, often called (although perhaps not strictly accurately) 進贅 (in Hokkien: Chin Choe) in which the bridegroom after marriage goes to live in his father-in-law's house (in normal marriages of course the bride goes to live in the bridegroom's house), but which do not involve his changing his surname. The family of the bride and the family of the bridegroom come to an agreement before the marriage as to whether the children of the marriage should adopt the surname of their father or the surname of their mother, or as to whether some of them should adopt the surname of one parent, and some that of the other.[11]

In southern China it seems that this 'chin choe' was not a permanent arrangement; Carstairs Douglas[12] states that under 'chin tsoe' the husband went to live in the house of the bride's father for a longer or shorter time, generally short.

---

[9] T'ien Ju-k'ang, 1956:23.

[10] Tan Chee-beng, 1988B:309-10. Doolittle (1868:69-70) does record the practice also in Hokchew (Fuzhou).

[11] I came across an example in 1955. Khor Ah Tiah had been married by 'Chin choi' into a family surnamed Tan. As a consequence (as it was put to me) "his children had to take the surname of his wife". He had a daughter called Yeow Sim, and she took the surname Tan. The custom is discussed by Freedman, 1957:122-3. The 'Chin Choay' marriage was a practice known to the Penang Baba community; the normal marriage was called 'chuah' (*Amoy* 'chhöa' "to marry a wife") (*Suara Baba* 1993, No.2:3).

[12] 1899:587.

Finally, a man or woman entering a Buddhist order will discard his (or her) own surname, and adopt one of the following to function as a surname:

Chinese	Mandarin	Hokkien	English
僧	Seng	Cheng	"A Buddhist Priest"[13]
釋	Shih	Sek	"Buddhism"

(being the first of the characters used for the transcription of the name for the Buddha - *Sakyamuni*).

At the same time, he or she will also take a new generation[14] and personal name. An example of this is afforded by the case of a Cantonese woman, a Bhuddhist nun, whose name is:

釋慧光　　(C6847-1979-0342) - Sek Wye Kwong

It is not known what her original surname was, before she became a nun and adopted 釋 Sek as her surname-in-religion. However, there are variations of this form, and this particular nun produced a letter received from China in which she was addressed like this:

慧光傅　　(C1979-0342-0265) - Wye Kwong Fu

It will be seen that the writer has not addressed her by her religious surname 釋 Sek, but has used merely her personal names Wye Kwong and suffixed to them a polite title 傅 'Fu', meaning 'a teacher'.

Taoist priests however retain their own family names.[15]

---

[13] Rattenbury relates that the mother of a sick baby was advised by her neighbours that the only way to save his life was to give him to a monastery. The baby's surname was changed from Wong to Tseng, as "Every monk's name is Tseng . . . " (Rattenbury, 1946:119).

Doolittle asserts that the act of adoption in itself fostered protection for a sickly or puny son. "His real parents imagine that the gods will let him live if his parents think so little of him as to allow him to be adopted into another family, on the principle that he must be a worthless or an indifferent lad." Doolittle, 1868:509.

[14] The generation name is however "of the Buddha system of genealogy", not showing actual blood descent — Kiang Kang-hu, 1934:143.

[15] See Kiang Kang-hu, 1934:143.

The Changing of given names

The reluctance to change the surname is compensated by an unusual readiness to change the given names. According to the old Chinese custom, the end of the first complete month of a child's existence was of particular significance – Doolittle observes that it was the time at which, in theory at least, the mother and child left the bedroom for the first time after her confinement, and it was marked also by the shaving of the child's head for the first time; this, too, was the recognized occasion for naming the child, the name being selected by the paternal grandfather if he was still living, otherwise by the father of the child.[16]

This custom probably accounts in part for the fact that many of the birth certificates of Chinese born in Malaysia showed the child as being unnamed, since the birth would generally be registered within a few days of its occurrence, although the laws of the Straits Settlements and most of the Malay States provided for free registration of the birth within fourteen days and permitted registration without fear of prosecution up to forty-two days from the date of the birth. The Registrar of Births and Deaths in Singapore has informed me that this is still (in 1996) the practice in Singapore.

In Malaysia nowadays, however, it is quite usual for the name for a Chinese child to be selected within a few days of birth, or sometimes even before birth; even so, the 'Full-month' ritual may still be performed, (with the distribution of red-coloured eggs and pulut rice) and at this time the name chosen for the child will be re-affirmed in front of the family altar.

The name first given to a child is known generally by one of the following terms:

Chinese	Mandarin	Hokkien	English
童子名	T'ung Tzu Ming	Tong Chu Beng	Child name
乳名	Ju Ming	Ju Mia^n	Milk name

---

[16] In the Penang *Sunday Gazette* of 21 January 1951, *Wu Liu* describes the Full Month ritual of a Cantonese living in Penang; in that case the month-old child had not yet been named — a couple of names had been selected by a fortune-teller but the final choice between them was to be left to the Goddess of Mercy, to whom the child had been given 'in adoption'.

奶名	Nai Ming	Nai Mia^n	Milk name
家中名	Chia Chung Ming		Name-in-the-family
小名	Hsiao Ming		Small name[17]

This starts off as a pet name, for use by the family and close friends, but it may so happen that a person will go through life and never have any other name. But if on becoming adult a man takes a new name "the *ming*, the personal name given at the third month, is used as a private and secret appellation";[18] this refers to the practice in China.

Mean Names (*Called in Mandarin*: Cho Ming 濁名)[19]

We have seen already that a surname can mean more to a Chinese than it does generally to his Western counterpart; at this point it may be convenient to examine the special significance which a personal name may also hold for the more superstitious element of the Chinese population. On this question, I cannot do better than to quote the views of Dr. de Groot. In relation to the 'Identification of Beings with their Images' he writes:[20]

> "It is a well-known characteristic of simple minds to associate, more or less intensively, representations with the beings these call to mind. The thought of a living personality, which a representation arouses, is strong enough to keep out the idea that the latter is mere lifeless matter. In particular this must be so in China, where all lifeless matter passes for animated, and, besides, no established knowledge exists of law and cause, so that no distinction between possible and impossible can be made."

---

[17] More information on these names can be found in Mathews' Dictionary, under characters 3144, 4524 & 4613; in Giles' Dictionary, characters Nos.5691 & 7940; in Dyer Ball, pp.113,114,397; in Bauer, 1959:12; in Creamer, 1995:910; and in Watson, 1986:621.

[18] Granet (1930:326)

[19] 'Choh ming' is given by De Groot, Vol.6, p.1131; I have not found the two words in this combination elsewhere. 'choh' corresponds to Amoy 'tak' (Carstairs Douglas, p.472) or 'lô' (Carstairs Douglas, p.314) meaning "muddy".

[20] De Groot, Vol.4, p.339.

Later,[21] he quotes examples from Chinese mythology of spectres having been put to flight when their names were pronounced; and remarks on the existence of writings which acquainted man with spectres and their names, with the object of affording protection from those beings. He continues:

"In fact then a name and its owner are identical[22]; it represents his body, his life, soul and energy, just as well as his image[23] and his horoscope do, considering the extreme consequence ... to which such assimilation leads and of which black art is the principal. We may here recall the fact that the name of a dead man, inscribed on his ancestal tablet or on his tombstone, actually represents his soul, so that, if it is effaced from the latter, the grave is no longer inhabited by his soul, but a powerless thing, devoid of shen or ling, useless as an object of worship and sacrifice. Knowing the names of spectres, man may pronounce them in his spells with emphasis and maledictions, and thus enhance the efficacy of the latter; he may to the same end inscribe them in his exorcising charms. Exorcists and prests therefore owe much of their power and influence among the people to their knowledge of the names of spectres; and this knowledge is in many cases the result of their capacity to see spectres ..."

---

[21] Vol.6, p.1125 et seq.

[22] Contrast western philosophical tradition, which abjures this notion; as Socrates expresses it ". . . how ridiculous would be the effect of names on things, if they were exactly the same with them! For they would be the doubles of them, and no one would be able to determine which were the names and which were the realities" (B. Jowett, ed. *The Dialogues of Plato*, Vol.1, Oxford: The Clarendon Press, 1892, p.379.)

[23] Here we may consider the traditional Chinese kitchen god, who may be found represented by an image of wood, or clay, or metal or stone. But often the image is replaced by writing his name or title on a piece of paper, which amounts to the same thing. (De Bruin, 1918:29.)

V. The Changing of Names

> If man may fight and even vanquish spectres by knowing their names, it is evident that, conversely, the world of darkness may injure and murder men by knowing theirs ..."[24]

(Here de Groot goes on to make reference to the tale of a man named Wang, of the Sung Dynasty, who succeeded in capturing a spectre which had on three successive days mischievously made a hole in a crab-weir which Wang had constructed in a canal. While Wang was carrying it home, with the avowed intention of burning it, the spectre besought repeatedly to learn Wang's family name and personal names; Wang was shrewd enough to refuse to divulge his name, whereupon the being muttered: 'he does not let me free, nor does he give me his names, what then can I contrive to do? if he only answers, he is a dead man'. Maintaining his silence until he reached home, Wang kindled a fire and burned the spectre, which was thus permanently laid.[25]) De Groot continues (p.1128):

> "... To this day the Chinese assert, that it is by no means rare for people of either sex to hear their names pronounced in the air and to incur a serious disease, and even death, not long after.
>
> It is then clear that the Chinese must feel and manifest an aversion from pronouncing names, especially their own and those of persons whom they are bound to esteem, to respect and to love. But the use of names of some sort cannot possibly be banished from daily life and conversation. It is therefore wise and sage to use as personal names such terms as denote in the ears of the uninitiated spectre-world quite other things, preferably despicable things which are not worth attending to; in other terms, naming men must be overt depreciation, or even scolding. Indeed, spectres will, on hearing such names, believe at once that the bearers are despised by everyone, and they will turn their refined maliciousness against persons of more importance.

---

[24] In this connection it is worth noting that in Malaysia a Malay child will often use his own name in place of "I", but a Chinese will always use the pronoun (e.g. 'goa'), thus avoiding use of his own personal name.

[25] De Groot, 1907, Vol.5, p.666

The Chinese are unanimous in their opinion that such names avert disease and mortality from children, and remarkably reduce the difficulties connected with their fosterage. Babies in particular cannot dispense with them, their strength being so small, their vitality so weak, their bodies so frail and so liable to injury by evil spirits."

De Groot gives a number of examples from Chinese history to show that the practice of conferring these 'mean names' on children dates from the most ancient times, and has not been confined to the lower classes; here are three such:

> Ch'ing, the ruler of the state of Tsin who died in 599BC, was named 黑臀 Black rump. – His successor King, who died in 580, bore the name of 獳 Angry dog or Mad dog ... in 300BC a prince of the name 蟻虱 Ant-louse, became a candidate for the throne in the state of Han ..."

Doolittle records that some parents, wishing to procure good health and longevity for a son "apply various sorts of derogatory names or epithets to him, as "Buddhist priest", "beggar", "refuse", "dirt", imagining that he will thus be allowed to live, and that no evil spirit or influence will injure his health."[26]

Writing of China in more recent times Williams writes: "Children are often given the name of an animal, and provided with a silver dog-collar 狗圈 [kou ch'üan] or ring, which is pressed over the head in order to induce evil spirits to imagine that the child is really an animal, and therefore not worth their attention".[27]

Berkowitz et al., report the practice in the Hong Kong New Territories: At the age of one month "the child is shaved and given a personal name, usually one of abuse, by the maternal uncle in the hope that the child will not attract evil spirits."[28]

Rattenbury relates that such 'mean' names are also used in addressing a child with the same protective intent: "Quite often a woman will call her son a little devil, not because she's angry with

---

[26] Doolittle, 1868:96.

[27] Williams, 1932:61; cf. Doré, 1914:11.

[28] Berkowitz et al., 1969:106.

him but because she loves him very much and wants to conceal his lovableness from the evil spirits."[29]

Dyer Ball reports another ruse formerly practised in China to protect a child, namely "his head may be shaved and he be called 'Buddhist priest'."[30]

The fact that the strange custom of giving derogatory names to children is still practised to the present day in Malaysia seems to suggest a continuing respect for malevolent spirits, and it is by no means unusual to meet a person whose name is, to say the least, less than flattering. A few examples of such names can be given:

Chinese	Mandarin	Hokkien	English
亞狗	A Kou	Ah Kau	A dog
狗屎	Kou Shih	Kau Sai	Dog excrement
亞豬	A Chu	Ah Ti	A Pig[31]
亞臭	A Ch'ou	Ah Chhau	Rotten
亞賤	A Chien	Ah Chian	Mean & worthless[32]

To continue the quotation from de Groot[33]:

"It is especially boys that receive such debasing names; indeed girls are not so valuable, on account of the fact that they do not strengthen and perpetuate the family, since, in obedience to the social law of exogamy, they are to go from home to marry in other tribes. And it is weak, unhealthy and

---

[29] Rattenbury, 1946:121.

[30] Dyer Ball, 1900:398.

[31] "The term *Chu*, pig, is commonly used as a Chinese surname, in the belief that the evil spirits will imagine a person so named is actually an animal, and therefore not worthy of attention." Williams, 1932:322. I have found no other reference to this practice, and find it surprising. Indeed I have not found 'Chu' (M1357) occurring in any list of Chinese surnames. Can he mean personal name?

[32] Lin Shan (1994:9) explains the choice of names such as "foolish", "naive like a child" etc. as conveying the parents' indifferent regard for worldy gains, and reflecting their philosophical attitude towards life; this is not in accord with other sources on the subject.

[33] Vol.6, p.1129; a more recent report of this practice can be found in Watson, 1986:621.

only sons in particular who are thus dubbed; many who require no extraordinary attention and care because they grow and thrive well, are exempted from such manifestation of affection."

In Malaysia, to complete the deception, the male child may be dressed in female clothes for a while, and his ears may be pierced for earrings.[34] As an instance of the use of a female name by a man, I once met a Teochew man whose name was 黄乙妹 spelt Ooi Yit Mooi. The last name Mooi means 'younger sister', and is naturally borne more often by girls than boys, but in his case no doubt served to protect him from the attentions of malicious spirits. He was not able to explain exactly why he had a woman's name: he knew merely that when he was born, in Poo Leng district, his grandfather, (who was illiterate), took him along to the local schoolmaster to choose a suitable name for him, and the schoolmaster advised that he would grow up to be strong if given a woman's name. De Groot shows that this custom, again, is an ancient one:

"Names expressing the female sect have been borne by male persons in all ages, and even in very ancient times. The prince who ruled the state of Lu from 721 to 710 before our era and is known in history by the posthumous name Yin, bore the name 息姑 the second character of which means a paternal aunt or mother-in-law. - The writings of Mencius mention one 馮婦 a famous tiger-hunter, whose personal name 婦 means Married wife .... The Books of the Later Han Dynasty mention an immortal being by the name of 魯女生 in which we see the character 女 or female ..."

So much for the reasons which cause some Chinese to give uncomplimentary names to their sons. Now, of the people having such unpleasant names some, especially the poorer and less educated people, will be content to use them for the rest of their

---

[34] I was first told about this by Mr Goh Keng Hui, my teacher in Singapore. The custom is of course known in China: "An ear-ring [êrh to] is sometimes attached to a child's ear to delude the evil spirits — always on the look-out to injure male children — into the belief that the boy is really a girl" Williams, 1932:61. The custom is discussed also by Dorè, 1914:15-16.

lives; but others, as they grow older, feel unhappy about having such names, and they seek something more fitting; if possible, they will choose a new name which is similar in pronunciation to the old, but which has a less derogatory meaning.

A common example of this is afforded by the name Ah Kau ('a dog') given above; people who have this name, on reaching maturity, may prefer to be known by the name 亞九 which is pronunced just the same, but which means 'Nine'. Again, there was a boy, a Hokkien, whose parents gave him the name Khiap-Si, or 'Ugly'. He grew up to be an educated young man, and chose for himself this name, which is pronounced similarly, but has a more agreeable meaning:

Chinese	Mandarin	Hokkien	English
俠士	Hsia Shih	Khiap-Su	'Knight Errant'

It may happen that a child which does not already have a 'mean name' shows itself to be unusually prone to sickness; in order to deter the fever-spectres from further unwelcome attentions, the parents will sometimes remedy the omission, and select a 'mean name', which will thereafter be used by the child. If, on the other hand, the sick child already has a 'mean name', the parents may try to change its fortune by selecting for it an auspicious name, in the hope that this will influence its destiny for the better; such a name, sometimes given to baby girls, is:

Chinese	Mandarin	Hokkien	English
好飼	Hao Szu	Ho Chhi	'Good-tempered and healthy'

Even adults may resort to the device of changing their names if they feel that their fortunes are not prospering sufficiently, again with the intention of deceiving the unfriendly spirits as to their identity, but this practice is not very usual in Malaysia. That it is long-standing in China is shown by the following quotation from de Groot[35]:

"Improving the fortune by changing the name is an old custom. About sixteen hundred years ago Koh Hung wrote:

---

[35] Vol.6, p.1137.

'Lao-tsze has often changed the names which he bore in his childhood and maturity, and Tan was not the only name he had. The following was the reason why he did so: the Canon of the Nine Divisions of the World and of the Numbers Three and Five, as also the *Yuen ch'en king*, say that there are in every human life conjunctions of dangers; and when these conjunctions occur, life may be prolonged and dangers overcome by changing the names of childhood and maturity, and thus remaining in concordance with the Universal Breath. Even at the present day many persons who have the Tao act in this wise'.

On the antiquity of the ancient traditions associated with the importance of discovering names, specifically as regards Taoist priests, we may consult more recent writings; Anna Seidel writes (1983:320,323):

"... the depiction and naming of supernatural beings already had a long tradition before the Han and was to become a central concern in Taoism later on."

She continues: (I have added the italics):

"To trace the layout of the land, to have fixed in a diagram the correct position of the heavenly bodies, to perceive the images of ancient sovereigns and to have insight into their succession in past and future, *and finally, to possess the secret names of nature gods and demons* – all these powers over Heaven and Earth, over space and time, are given to the sovereign who rightfully owns the Script and Chart. ... *The Taoist priests likewise are initiated into the secret names* and likenesses of the gods and demons of the universe and they have the power to summon their help and to subdue them should they be maleficent."

Pursuing the same point Boltz (1994:132-3) refers to "a belief that by naming or depicting images of demons and supernatural creatures one could exercise control over them, preventing the occurrence of untoward events, and blocking the malevolent effects of their demonic influences".

He goes on to observe "A natural extension of the belief that drawing a picture of a demon is a preventive measure to ward off its malevolent effects would be that writing the demon's name

86

could serve the same prophylactic purpose". We are given grounds to conclude indeed that the earliest studies of Chinese language may have been motivated by a desire to control names.

These more recent scholarly publications serve to support the testimony given to us by De Groot a century ago, and at the same time emphasize once more the crucial significance of names in Chinese csociety from the earliest times.

The custom of changing names to influence fortune is not exclusively Chinese. It is known amongst the Siamese too;[36] and its practice by the Malays is referred to by Sir Richard Winstedt: 'Even today, many Malays have four different names, the name given in infancy, a name given to mislead the spirits of disease, a name given on marriage, a name given after the pilgrimage to Mecca'[37].

School names

When a child enters his first school, his teacher may give him a new name, possibly chosen with reference to some particular aptitude or characteristic which he displays; such names may be known variously as:

Chinese	Mandarin	Hokkien	English
書名	Shu Ming	Su Mia^n	'Book name'; or
册名	Ts'e Ming	Chheh Mia^n	'Book name'; or
學名	Hsueh Ming	Oh Mia^n	'School name'

Some people will use this school name not only during their careers at school, but also for social and business activities as

---

[36] See for example J.H.C.S. Davidson (ed.) 1987. *Lai Su' Thai, Essays in honour of E.H.S. Simmonds*. University of London, p.41.

[37] In JMBRAS, 17, (3), 1939:41. Two more examples may be given : F. Steingass, A *Comprehensive Persian-English Dictionary* (1957, p.1378): "näm gardänïdan, To change one's name (done with a sick person, in the superstitious belief of securing thereby his recovery)"; or M. Covarrubias, *Island of Bali* (1937, p.131) A child's name "has an influence over his life and should he become sick often, the name is to blame and a more appropriate one is chosen by the priest or the witch-doctor".

adults; in short, for all purposes outside the family circle. To take an example from real life:

There was a man born in China (Hokkien Province) round about 1920 whose name originally was:

謝 慶 治	Chiah Kheng Tee
6200-1987-3112	(Kheng was a generation name)

When he started school, his teacher gave him a new name, and he became:

謝 澄 淵	Chiah Teng Eng
6200-3397-8673	That is the name which he uses now.

It will be observed that the examples given in the preceding paragraphs concern the changing of given names only, the surname remaining unchanged.

Marriage names
According to Cantonese custom, a bridegroom adopts a special 'marriage name' for use on his wedding day only. It is called:

Chinese	Mandarin	Hokkien	English
字格	Tzu Ke	Ji Keh	'Name frame'

This name will consist of the bridegroom's actual surname, plus two given names chosen for the occasion by his father. The name is inscribed and framed, and hangs on the wall of the house for the day. The first given name so chosen for an elder brother will also be used on the occasion of the marriage of his younger brothers. The second given name will of course be different for each brother. Van der Sprenkel states that both bride and groom take a 'tzu' as a marriage name. Rubie S. Watson on the other hand records that women lose their personal name when they marry.[38]

Mention may be made also of the other types of name which may be adopted by Chinese:

---

[38] Van der Sprenkel, 1963:168; Watson, Rubie S., 1986:619.

The 'Fancy name'

This is a somewhat inadequate translation for the Chinese term

Chinese	Mandarin	Hokkien	English
號	Hao	Ho	A mark, sign, designation &c.

This is a fancy name adopted by a man himself or given to him by his friends, and like the school name often bears some reference to his pursuits or character. Writing about Chinese scholars, Lin Yutang (1947:383) observes: "In the course of life, as their taste develops and their wisdom deepens, they often take a fancy to a certain word or phrase fraught with meaning, and give themselves another name to indicate their spiritual progress or a particularly meaningful experience: hence a person may have several *hao* or fancy names ...".

If a man adopts more than one 'Fancy name', the additional name will known as 別號 Pieh Hao 'Another name'. (Col. Burkhardt renders this term 'Studio name'.)[39]

A 外號 Wai-Hao is a nickname or intimate name.

The 'Tzu'

Chinese	Mandarin	Hokkien
字	Tzu[4]	Ju

which is sometimes known as the 字名 (Tzu Ming). The authorities are not unanimous on the precise meaning of this. Gile's definition (1912, no.12,324) is "A name or style taken at the age of twenty, which may be used by friends, or of one another by brothers". Dyer Ball[40] writes "On marriage the young man takes still another name, his style or 'great name' . . ." Couvreur refers to the Tzu as being the name given during adolescence.[41] Alan R. Priest writes: "The Chinese also use another intimate name, the Tzu (字)[42] (sometimes absurdly and meaninglessly translated as

---

[39] Vol.2, p.191.

[40] Dyer Ball, 1900:397.

[41] Couvreur, 1916:582. "... désigné par son 字 *tséu* nom reçu dans l'adolescence".

[42] *Pinyin* 'zì'; see Creamer, 1995:910.

'Style') which is created in much the same manner as the Hao, except that it properly carries some direct literary allusion to the Ming,[43] and is in its use somewhat more elegant and formal than the Hao". A commentary on the Chinese Book of Etiquette and Ceremonial observes "the Style takes the place, on the lips of outsiders, of the name his parents gave him, and leaves the latter for the parents' own use".[44]

'Flowery names'

The descriptive nicknames which are fairly common in Malaysia are known in Chinese as:

Chinese	Mandarin	Hokkien	English
華名	Hua Ming	Hoe Mia^n	'Flowery name'

or less frequently may be known as

藝名	I Ming	Ge Mia^n	'Fancy name'

A few examples of this kind of sobriquet:

Chinese	Mandarin	Hokkien	English
大目	Ta Mu	Toa Bak	'Big eyes'
大肥林	Ta Fei Lin	Toa Pui Lim	'Big fat Lim'
跛足林	Po Tsu Lin	Pai Kha Lim	'Lame Lim'

Dyer Ball notes that such nicknames often incorporate 'Ah' in them, such as 'Ah Pin' (meaning Flat-nose)[45].

The term I Ming 藝名 is often used to denote a stage-name, or a pen-name or the pseudonym used by an artist. Some examples will be found under the head 'Journalists' on page 98, below.

---

[43] In ancient China, there was usually some link of meaning between the 'ming' and the 'tzu'. For example two men with 耕 M3343 'kêng' "to plough" in their 'ming' had 牛 M4737 'niu' "ox" in their 'tzu' (Boodberg, P.A., 1940, 5,131).

[44] Steele, 1917, Vol.I, p.264.

[45] Dyer Ball, 1900:398.

Official names

These are known to the Chinese by one of the following terms:

Chinese	Mandarin	Hokkien	English
官名	Kuan Ming	Koan Mia^n	'Official name' - 'Koan' is an official or a mandarin
考名	K'ao Ming	Kho Mia^n	'Examination name'

Giles (p.799) defines this as "the 'official' or distinctive name, given at the age of 15 or 16. It is this name which appears, with the surname, on visiting cards, and by which a man is officially known, but it is not correctly used in speaking either to or of its owner". Such names are not encountered in present-day Malaysia.

Posthumous names

After a man's death he may be known by a posthumous name. In Malaysia, however, posthumous names are rarely if ever used, and a person will be known after his death by the name which he used during his lifetime.

Girls

This surfeit of names is not enjoyed by women, and girls, to quote Dyer Ball "have to be content with a milk name, a marriage name, and nicknames"[46]. The sexual inequality in the matter of names is discussed fully by Rubie S. Watson (1986).

Aversion to persons having identical names

There is a Chinese prejudice against a given name (that is, any component of the name other than the surname) being identical with any of the given names of the parent or the grandparent, or great grandparent, or even more remote ancestor[47]: Dyer Ball mentions a curious case long ago when the 'Peking Gazette' recorded an application from General Hsieh Hung-chang in

---

[46] Dyer Ball, 1900:400.

[47] We have seen (p.15 above) that Van der Sprenkel (1963:167) mentions a cycle of five generation names, in which each name would recur after five generations; this sounds extraordinary, and I have not come across any reference to it in any other source.

Canton to change one of his names "as it had been discovered from his family register that a remote ancestor of his had a name identical with his own".[48] Having identical names would amount to disrespect, inasmuch as it would be a failure to observe the proper distance which separates the earlier generations from the later.

It may happen that a son may be given a name identical in western spelling with that of one of his father's given names, but it will nearly always be found that the Chinese characters of the names are not identical, and that the pronunciation in Chinese will be different. For example, there is a Hokkien man called Ng Kee Lang 黃襆弄 (7806-??-1702) who has a son named Ng Kee Lin 黃其仁 (7806-0366-0088). It will be seen that the name 'Kee' which occurs in the names of the father and son has different Chinese characters, although the difference is not shown when the names are reduced to western spelling.

However, a fashion has grown up in recent years in Malaysia which contradicts this custom: a father will sometimes give one of his own names to a son, preceded by the word 小 (*Mand.*: Hsiao, *Hok.*: Sio) meaning small. For example, there is a man named:

| 楊德明 | (2799-1795-2494) Yeoh Teik Beng; wishing to pass on one of his personal names to one of his sons he may name him: |
| 楊小德 | (2799-1420-1795) Yeoh Sio Teik |

Similarly, a woman with the name:

| 楊亞蓮 | (2799-0068-5571) Yeoh Ah Lian, might call her daughter: |
| 陳小蓮 | (7115-1420-5571) Tan Sio Lian |

Burkhardt[49] writes 小 that Hsiao is the northern equivalent for 亞 Ah (used south of the Yangtze), both being merely honorific prefixes for the sake of euphony, (a comment which bears on our earlier remarks on the middle name (p.21).

---

[48] Dyer Ball, 1900:220.

[49] Vol.2, p.191.

In fact 'Sio' is definitely known in southern China, and there are indications that it is used by Teochews. One man who used it had a son born in Swatow in 1909. The father's name was

郭迪懷	(C6753-6611-2037)	Kuo Ti Huai (in Md. pronunciation); he named a son
郭小懷	(C6753-1420-2037)	Kuo Hsiao Huai; in fact the son preferred to use as his middle name 少 (C1421) Shao, which he felt had more literary connotations.[50]

To consider another apparent contradiction: there is a man whose name is 陳文榜 (7115-2429-2831) Tan Boon Pong, and who has a son called 陳文和 (7115-2429-0735) Tan Boon Hoe; the Chinese character for 文 Boon in each case is identical, and at first sight it appears to be a clear contradiction of the proposition just put forward; but the rather special use of 文 Boon has been remarked upon earlier (page 21), and if we regard it here as an addition to compensate for the lack of a middle name rather than as a name in its own right, it may not really be a contradiction after all.

Similarly the example below of the name of a father and son whose middle name in each case is 亞 'Ah', a word which I think should be regarded as a familiar appellation rather than as a personal name:

Father - 陳亞奎 Tan Ah Kei (7115-0068-1145)	A Henghwa father and
Son - 陳亞獅 Tan Ah Sai (7115-0068-3740)	son living in Kelantan

I have come across cases which appear more positively to contradict the thesis that a son or daughter should not be given a personal name identical with one of the personal names of the

---

[50] Both Hsiao and Shao are common Chinese personal names, see Lin Shan, 1994:116,93.

parents. I have heard (indirectly through a foster-son) of a man in the Lam Oa district, Hokkien Province, whose name was:

高德時　　　(7559-1795-2514) Ko Teik See

and whose father had an identical middle name:

高德海　　　(7559-1795-3189) Ko Teik Hai

To give another example, there lives in Kelantan a Cantonese goldsmith called:

黃連富　　　(7806-6647-1381) Wong Lian Foo

His mother's name is:

吳連香　　　(0702-6647-7449) Ng Lian Hiong

When contemplating these apparent contradictions we may keep two considerations in mind. One is the possibility that in a community where not everyone is literate in Chinese, the Chinese characters of names may be written erroneously. The second point is to note that with one exception the examples above postulate the identity of the *first* given name; and we have seen (p.21 above) that it is the *second* given name which appears to be the real personal name, and that is where the identity of names would be more significant. Some examples of these will be given below.

When a Chinese woman marries, she is regarded as leaving her own family and joining that of her husband; after marriage, her loyalties will be primarily to her husband's parents, rather than to her own. If it happens that the bride at the time of marriage has a personal name which is the same as one of the personal names of her parents-in-law, or of their parents, she will be obliged to change it. If for example there is a woman named:

葉金枝　　　(5509-6855-2655) Yap Kim Kee who is about to be married, and the name of the father of her husband-to-be is:

曾寶金　　　(2582-1405-6855) Chan Po Kim, she will be obliged to abandon the name 'Kim' in favour of some other name. She may for example change her name to:

葉璇枝　　　(5509-3872-2655) Yap Soan Kee

If it happens that one of the personal names of the bride-to-be is identical with one of the personal names of the man she is to marry, she may similarly change it; but in this case the rule is not so rigidly enforced - for instance, there is a Hainanese couple whose names are:

Husband:	林鴻華	(C 2651-7703-5478)	- Lim Hong Hua
Wife:	翁麗華	(C 5040-7787-5487)	- Ong Lee Hua

the wife has retained the name 'Hua' after her marriage. As another example of a man and wife having identical personal names, the elderly Teochew man mentioned earlier (see p.82) called:

黃乙妹	7806-0044-1188: Ooi Yit Mooi, has a wife called
陳如妹	7115-1172-1188: Tan Joo Moy; (Moy being the same Chinese character as the husband's name Mooi)

When asked about this phenomenon, the husband said that he married his wife in the Poo Leng District in 1916, and he had never heard of the customary changing on marriage of any name which is identical with that of the husband.

Needless to say, one will also meet names of a husband and wife where the western spelling of one of the personal names of each person will be identical; for example, there is a Hokkien couple with the names:

Husband:	黃天知　Ng Thian Tee (7806-1131-4249)	Although the last personal name of each is spelt 'Tee' the Chinese characters of the two are different.
Wife:	許掩治　Koh Yim Tee (6079-2237-3112)	

VI   Miscellaneous

The word 'Neoh'

This word is written in Chinese: - 娘 (C 1224) and is pronounced in
Mandarin 'Niang'. One dictionary definition of it reads "A girl; a
woman; a mother; a wife"; it will commonly be found written at the
end of the names of Hokkien and Teochew women, particularly
those connected with the Straits Settlements. Perhaps it should be
regarded as a title, but it is generally assumed to be a part of the
name of the individual; an argument for this is the fact that without
it the woman would often be left with only one element in her
personal name, which is unusual. On the other hand it certainly
appears to function as a title, something like "Madam". It may have
both functions.

Khoo Su Nin writes (in a personal communication) that 'Neoh'
is found as the last component of the names of Hokkien women on
Penang tombstones dating from the nineteenth century. She gives
her impression that it was frequently used before the Second World
War, and especially before 1900; and she adds "In common
Hokkien usage today, Neoh usually refers to "mother-in-law" or an
older woman with married children". Indeed it occurs as a loan-
word in Malay with the meaning "mother-in-law".

Here are some examples of its use:

Chinese	*Mandarin*	*In Hokkien*
李瑞蓮娘	Li Shui Lien Niang	Lie Soei Lian Nio
(C2621-3843-5571-1224)		(The Indonesian spelling
		is used for the Hokkien name)
陳鄔娘	Ch'en Wu Niang	Tan Poay Neoh
(C7115-6762-1224)		(This is the name of a
		Hokkien woman who has
		never been to Malaysia)

97

王娘 (C3769-1224)	Wang Niang	Ong Neoh (A woman resident in China. Probably she has a proper personal name, but her name was written like this in an official form; she had never been to Malaysia)

The name 'Mek'

This name is often given to Malay girls; it is particularly common in Kelantan, where it is also used as a form of address to a girl whose name is not known. Chinese who have been long settled in Kelantan sometimes give it to their daughters.

It seems to be generally represented in Chinese by the word 脈 (C5181, meaning 'the pulse'), which is pronounced 'Mê' or 'Mai' in Mandarin and 'Meh' in Hokkien. Some examples may be given:

梁脈泉 2733-5181-3123	Liong Mek Suan	(A Hainanese woman, born and resident in Kelantan)
張脈細 1728-5181-4798	Teo Mek Se	(A Hokkien woman, born and resident in Kelantan)

黄脈光 7806-5181-0342	Ng Mek Kooi	)
李脈南 2621-5181-0589	Lee Mek Lam	) All resident in the) State of Kelantan
陳脈心 7115-5181-1800	Tan Mek Sim	)

Journalists

Chinese newspaper writers often preserve their anonymity by using pen names. Examples of such pen-names seen in the local Malaysian Chinese press:

Chinese	Mandarin	Hokkien	Translation in English
向 西 (0686-6007)	Hsiang Hsi	Hiong Se	Facing westwards
東南方 (2639-0589-2455)	Tung Nan Fang	Tong Lam Hong	South-easterly

金石 (6855-4258)	Chin Shih	Kim Chioh	Golden stone
海雲 (3189-7189)	Hai Yun	Hai Hun	Sea clouds

It seems that few contributors to the Chinese press care to have works published under their own names; some, not content with one pen-name, may use a number of such names, so that it is said that sometimes a writer looking at an old article signed with a pen-name cannot even be sure whether he was the author or not.

Henghwa names

Chinese from Henghwa, in Hokkien Province, sometimes have names which do not conform to the usual Chinese pattern; a few examples of these curious names may be given as a matter of interest:

Chinese	*Henghwa*
李西面妹 (C2621-6007-7240-1188)	Lee Say May Mui (Literally: surname Lee - 'west' - 'face' - 'younger sister'; Presumably a woman who in China lived in the western side of the house)
李氏前面妹 (C2621-3044-0467-7240 -1188)	Lee See Cheng Bin Moy (Literally: surname Lee - madam - frontside - younger sister; perhaps she lives in the front of the house in China) (her son is surnamed Lau)
李後產妹 (C2621-1775-3934-1188)	Lee Au Sung Moi (Literally: surname Lee - Later-born-younger sister; it is the name of an elderly man)
陳山里狗 (C7115-1472-6849-3699)	Tan Shaw Lee Kow ("Dog-of-the-hills - Tan") However, when he had been residing for some years in Malaya he was using a

"normal" Chinese name (still retaining the same surname of course)

陳文富
(C7115-2429-1381)

Tan Boon Hoo

蔡啞口婆
(C5591-0800-0656-1237)

Sai Ah Kow Por
(Literally: surname Sai-dumb-mouth-old woman; she was an elderly widow, whose late husband's surname had been 李 Lee)

These names, which appeared on applications for entry permits in respect of persons resident in China, are quoted merely because they are oddities, and departures from the general rule; people of the Henghwa dialect group who take up residence in Malaysia use the conventional surname and personal name combination just like other Chinese.

Mentioning the names of the dead
More conservative Chinese will refrain from mentioning the personal names of a deceased relative, a convention probably originating in the belief, remarked upon in the preceding chapter, that concealment of a person's name promotes his safety from the unwelcome attentions of malevolent spirits. They will not, naturally enough, refrain from mentioning his surname. On this point the Confucian philosopher Mencius is quoted as saying:

> "We avoid the personal name of the deceased, but not his surname. The surname is something he has in common with others; the personal name is peculiar to him."[1]

Deities
Deities usually have titles only. "A god is ...never known by personal and family name."[2] But sometimes they are — Anna Seidel (1983:322) refers to "the gods of the Five Sacred Peaks",

---

[1] See De Groot, Vol.VI:1141, note 4. Giles cites much the same thing (G4599) "the surname is common (to the clan), the personal name belongs to the individual".

[2] Feuchtwang, 1992:82.

and the "Ocean gods of the four orients" as having family and personal names (*hsing* and *ming*).

Plurality of names

To add to the confusion arising from the use of different personal names by one person in the different stages of his life, some Chinese businessmen make a practice of using a different name for each separate sphere of their activities.[3]

Illegitimate children

Under Chinese custom these are regarded as being the property of the mother, and they nearly always take the mother's surname.

Marriage prohibition

> *"To marry a girl of your own surname*
> *It is a great sin and also a shame."* [4]

Chinese custom (it is on record that the practice goes back as far as the Chou Dynasty, possibly 3,000 years ago), will not permit marriage between a man and woman having identical surnames; Staunton's translation of the Chinese law *Ta Tsing Lü Li* (大清律例) reads:

> "Whenever any persons having the same family name inter-marry, the parties and the contractor of the marriage shall each receive sixty blows, and the marriage shall be null and void, the man and woman shall be separated, and the marriage presents forfeited to government."[5]

---

[3] Dyer Ball (1900:400) records this practice in southern China a century ago.

[4] Tan Pow Tek.1924:88.

[5] According to Boulais' translation "the wife shall return to her family ..." (Boulais, G., 1923. *Manuel du Code Chinois* ... Shanghai: Catholic Mission, p.277.) De Groot observes: "In that country not only the moral law still stigmatizes all marriages between persons who have the same family name, as unpardonable incest. Also under the written law of the kingdom it is forbidden on pain of dissolution and sixty strokes." — De Groot, 1885:106.

The rather severe penalties for this infringement of the old law have never had force in Malaysia, and indeed the current (1950) marriage law of China contains no prohibition of the marriage of a man and a woman having the same surname.[6]

Even so, custom dies hard, and such marriages are rare in Malaysia even today.[7] In Hong Kong the position is similar. Marriage with a person of one's own surname is considered improper. "... among Hakka people individuals with the same surname are assumed to be relatives and intermarriage is frowned upon, although it does occur occasionally".[8]

The question attracted attention also in the Netherlands Indies. Nio Joe Lan[9] writes of a true story in Indonesian literature about the problems of a young Chinese couple in Bandung who fell in love and married, even though they had the same surname. The event took place in 1917. In that year the Netherlands Indies Government actually promulgated a statute prohibiting marriage between Chinese persons of the same surname[10]. Nevertheless, Nio Joe Lan goes on to say that by the 1930s such marriages no longer attracted disapproval, and that they took place even in China; what had been taboo in 1917, had become accepted. This may not have been entirely true, for in about 1934 Oen Tjhing Tiauw published a play called *Doea keliroean*, in which the prohibition of marriage between two people of the same surname was criticized once more.[11]

---

[6] Although T'ien Ju-k'ang (1956:22) writes "In China the surname was until recently strictly exogamous, and remains so to a very marked degree, especially in rural districts and in the North".

[7] The marriage of persons with identical surnames was the subject of an article by *Wu Liu* in the Penang *Sunday Gazette* of 24 September 1950.

[8] Berkowitz et al., 1969:14.

[9] Nio Joe Lan, 1962. *Sastera Indonesia-Tionghoa*. Jakarta:Gunung Agung, 97-99. The author of the story 'Roesia Bandoeng' uses a pen name "Chabanneau".

[10] De Bruin, 1918:116. Art. 1333 of the statute dealt with this.

[11] Salmon, Claudine, 1981. *Literature in Malay by the Chinese of Indonesia*. Paris: Archipel, p.275.

But that the rule was not rigidly applied, even in the China at the close of the last century, is shown by the following remark of Giles,[12] "Broadly speaking, persons of the same surname may not marry. But in some cases it is tolerated, as for instance where a large area is occupied by a single clan. Then intermarriage is permitted, but it must not be between persons related within the five degrees of mourning. On the other hand, certain families (e.g. the 徐 and the 余) will not intermarry because their surnames, now different, were once the same." (The two surnames are Hsü, M2841 and Yü, M7605.)

This prohibition extends to persons of the same surname even if they belong to a different dialect group. Doolittle puts it very strongly: "*Males and females of the same family surname never intermarry in China* ... No matter how remote the relation between parties having the same ancestral name, and no matter if they be from distant provinces, and their ancestors have not known each other for hundreds or even thousands of years, they may not marry."[13] However, some Chinese say that in those circumstances the misconduct is not quite so serious.[14] Newell reports another instance of the amelioration of the rule: "In North China, in many instances, if the relation between the two parties to the marriage is not closer than three generations, then two parties with the same surname may get married by a subterfuge. This subterfuge is to alter one stroke in the character so that the surname is pronounced differently. However, this practice varies from place to place."[15]

Another circumstance may be mentioned where the prohibition is relaxed to some extent. It was mentioned on page 39 that a large proportion of Chinese Muslims bears the surname Ma: consequently a rigid prohibition of marriage between men and women bearing this surname is not practical, and in fact custom

---

[12] Giles, 1892, under character No.4599.

[13] Doolittle, 1868:69.

[14] Freedman, 1957:71.

[15] Newell, 1962:209.

sanctions the marriage of a Muslim man and woman bearing this surname provided that there is no near blood relationship.

The prohibition of marriage between persons having the same surnames is clearly ancient. A commentary on the Chinese *Book of Etiquette and Ceremonial* observes that such marriages "were forbidden on the eugenic ground that the offspring of such unions were bound to be unhealthy and short-lived".[16] According to Doolittle the Chinese said that marriages among those of the same ancestral name would "confound the human relations".[17]

Freedman discusses more scientifically some of the reasons given for this practice of exogamy by the Chinese. He goes so far as to assert that sociologically speaking "The Chinese surname may furnish a basis for the formation of associations, but its fundamental and well-nigh universal function is the control of marriage by the rule of surname exogamy." In other words he would harness the whole surname system into the service of surname exogamy.[18]

It has been pointed out that surname exogamy actually serves to promote links between surname groups, thus binding the Chinese together. "Each clan is exogamous, and every individual therefore has matrilateral relatives in one other clan . . . ".[19]

De Groot similarly sees the measure as a device to bring about links of blood relationship, thus furthering good relations between the different [single-surname] villages.[20]

Titles
Mention was made on page 40, above, of the use of titles T'ai T'ai 太太 (Mrs.) and 氏 Shih (Madam). The other polite titles in common use (for example, in the addresses on envelopes) are:

---

[16] Steele, 1917. Vol.I p.266.

[17] Doolittle, 1868:69.

[18] Freedman, 1957:72. He relates an illuminating little anecdote about the surprise of a Chinese on learning that the Malays do not have a surname system, and his puzzled question "Then how do they know whom not to marry ?"

[19] T'ien Ju-k'ang, 1956:29.

[20] De Groot, 1885:106.

Chinese	Mandarin	Hokkien	English
先生	Hsien Sheng	Sian Si^n	'Born earlier'; it also means 'teacher'

This is the equivalent of 'Mr.', and is placed after the surname or full name of men; e.g.

Chinese	Mandarin	Hokkien	English
王先生	Wang Hsien Sheng	Ong Sian Si^n	Mr. Wang
王永海先生	Wang Yung Hai Hsien Sheng	Ong Eng Hai Sian Si^n	Mr. Wang Yung Hai

and in respect of women, being equivalent to either 'Madam' (in respect of a married woman) or 'Ms' or 'Miss', the Chinese use:

Chinese	Mandarin	Hokkien	English
女士	Nu Shih	Lu Su	Originally a 'Female Teacher' or a 'Lady'.

This is used after the full maiden name, never with the surname only nor with the husband's surname; to take an example:

Chinese	Mandarin	Hokkien	English
符愛蓮女士	Fu Ai Lien Nu Shih	Hu Ai Lian Lu Su	Miss (or Madam) Fu Ai Lien

Examples of Chinese names, with comment on meaning
By now it has become clear that to a Chinese a name not only has great significance, it can decisively influence the future of the one who bears it. Granet (1930:249) puts the point strongly: "The name expresses the being, and makes the *destiny*, so that any man born a Prince will become a stable-boy if he has been given the name of "Ostler" while it is impossible that another should fail, who has been called 'He will succeed'."

But life in old China was never simple, and it was not only the name itself which could be auspicious or ominous. The story is told of a seventh son in ancient China who was persecuted because "seven" (七 Md Ch'ih) in his name sounded like (漆 Md

Ch'ih) meaning "lacquer", which is black, which in that context was regarded as sinister.[21]

Bauer discusses comprehensively the considerations which have governed the choice of personal names in history, and the categories into which personal names can be classified. He also gives a useful index to individual words used as names (in Chinese radical order).[22] Evelyn Lip's book explains in detail how auspicious names should be chosen, and she gives a list of Chinese names alphabetically arranged under the Pinyin spelling, together with the English meaning.[23] Lin Shan (1994) devotes a major part of his book to a list of Chinese names also alphabetically arranged under the Pinyin spelling, together with the English meaning.

In the light of this it may be of value to consider a number of typical names among those which are commonly found in Malaysia, to see how they are formed and how often more can be deduced from a name than first meets the eye.

Quite often, the spelling of a Chinese name is western writing will give an indication of the dialect-group to which it belongs; but this is not an infallible guide, as sometimes people use the pronunciation of the dialect which is predominant in the area in which they are living — for example, a Chinese living in Hong Kong will most likely spell his name in the Cantonese way, whether he himself is Cantonese or not. But generally speaking one can guess the dialect of a person from the spelling of his name. The sixty odd names considered below have been arranged under the main dialect groups — Hokkien, Cantonese, Hakka, Teochew, Hainanese and Kwongsai — but apart from that are not written in any particular order relative to each other. In each case a note has been made of the literal meaning of the characters in the names, but in respect of the surnames the literal meaning has no longer any real significance, and in respect of the personal

---

[21] Boodberg, 1939:272. The Amoy pronunciation of this word 'chhat' gives the Malay word 'cat' (for "paint").

[22] Bauer, 1959:254-374; the index to words is on pp.375-383.

[23] Evelyn Lip, 1994:164-173.

names the literal meaning given here will commonly be but a poor indication of the significance or allusion which so often underlies them.

Examples of the names of Hokkien people

謝木順 Cheah Bok Soon
6200-2606-7311
    (a man)

Cheah: To thank:
Bok: Wood;
Soon: Prosperous

呂珊 Loo Sung
0712-3790
    (a woman)

Loo: The name of an ancient state;
Sung: Coral

林金枝 Lim Kim Kee
1651-6855-2655
    (a man)

Lim: A forest;
Kim: Gold;
Kee: A branch.

(Note: The two elements for wood 木 and gold 金 occur in this name.)

陳亞九 Tan Ah Kow
7115-0068-0046
    (a man)

Tan: The name of an ancient states;
Ah: A familiar name; Kow: Nine;
(but possibly as a boy he was known by the character 狗, also pronounced, Kow, which means 'dog').

陳草頭 Tan Chaw Thow
7115-5430-7333
    (a trisha pedlar)

Tan: The name of an ancient state;
Chaw: Grass; Thow: Head.

(He says that this odd name was given to him by his mother when he was small; it could be derived from some peculiarity of his hair, but Chaw Thow also means grass-roots; or it could be that he was originally called 臭頭 (also Chaw Thow - 'scabby head', and changed his name).

陳反 Tan Huan
7115-0646
    (a woman)

Tan: The name of an ancient state;
Huan: To rebel.

張炳炎 Tio Peng Jam
1728-3521-3508
    (a man)

Tio: To draw a bow;
Peng: Bright;
Jam: Flames (pronounced Yam)

(The spelling Tio, instead of the more usual Teoh, and the spelling Jam for Yam both indicate a connection with Indonesia).

黄水木　Wong Swee Moh
7806-3055-2606
(a man)

Wong: Yellow;
Swee: Water (an element);
Moh: Wood (also an element).

(This name of a Hokkien man is spelt according to the Cantonese pronunciation; he comes from a Cantonese area in the state of Perak).

黄琴聲　Ooi Khim Seng
7806-3830-5116
(a man)

Ooi: Yellow;
Khim: A Chinese lute;
Seng: Sound

(A rather picturesque name: 'Sound of the Chinese lute').

莊西尿　Ch'ng Say Leoh
5445-6007-1443
(a man)

Ch'ng: Village or farm
Say: West
Leoh: Urine

(When asked about this odd name, he said that he had had it as long as he could remember, and had never had any other name; he was an elderly man, born in China.)

Examples of the names of Cantonese people

陳亞妹　Chan Ah Mui
7115-0068-1188
(a woman)

Chan: Name of an ancient state;
Ah: A familiar name;
Mui: Younger sister; the last indicates that this is the name of a female, although occasionally men may be called 'Mui'.

曾四妹　Cheng She Mooi
2582-0934-1188
(a woman)

Cheng: A surname;
She: Four;
Mooi: Younger sister.

(The name indicates that she is, probably, the fourth daughter in the family.)

鍾靜瓊　Chong Ching Kheng
6945-7234-3890
(a woman)

Chong: A goblet;
Ching: Peaceful;
Kheng: Beautiful.

張凌　　Chong Leng　　　Chong: To draw a bow;
1728-0407　　　　　　　　Leng: Pure.
　　　(a man)

馮亞二　Fong Ah Yee　　　Fong: A surname;
7458-0068-0059　　　　　Ah: A familiar name;
　　　(a woman)　　　　　Yee: Two
(She is probably the second daughter in the family.)

林女　　Lam Noi　　　　　Lam: A forest;
2651-1166　　　　　　　　Noi: A woman
　　　(a woman)
　　　(Naturally enough, this last name is usually used by
　　　women, although it may very occasionally be used by
　　　men.)

李三妹　Lee Sam Moy　　　Lee: Plums;
2621-0005-1188　　　　　Sam: Three;
　　　(a woman)　　　　　Moy: Younger Sister. (Possibly the
　　　　　　　　　　　　　third daughter in the family.)

劉根　　Low Kan　　　　　Low: A surname;
0491-2704　　　　　　　　Kan: Beginning, or foundation.
　　　(a man)

梁發　　Leong Fatt　　　　Leong: A bridge;
2733-4099　　　　　　　　Fatt: To send forth, to manifest;
　　　(a man)　　　　　　(No doubt in respect of wealth.)

吳金妹　Ng Kim Mooi　　　Ng: Name of an ancient state;
0702-6855-1188　　　　　Kim: Gold;
　　　(a woman)　　　　　Mooi: Younger sister.

黃三斤　Wong Sam Kun　　Wong: Yellow;
7806-0005-2443　　　　　Sam: Three;
　　　(a boy)　　　　　　Kun: A catty (weight).

楊亞二　Yeong Ah Yee　　　Yeong: The willow;
2799-0068-0059　　　　　Ah: A familiar name;
　　　(a woman)　　　　　Yee: Two.
　　　(Very probably the second daughter in a family.)

楊亞妹　Yong Ah Mui
2799-0068-1188
　　(a woman)

Yong: The willow;
Ah: A familiar name;
Mui: Younger sister.

A Cantonese family (Husband, wife, daughter, daughter):

陳興九　Chan Heng Kow
7115-5281-0046
　　(husband)

Chan: The name of an ancient state;
Heng: To prosper;
Kow: Nine.

潘二妹　Phoon Yee Mooi
3382-0059-1188
　　(wife)

Phoon: An affluent of the Han river;
Yee: Two;
Mooi: Younger sister.

陳愛　Chan Oi
7115-1947
　　(daughter)

Chan: The name of an ancient state;
Oi: Love, affection.

陳千　Chan Chin
7115-0578
　　(daughter)

Chan: The name of an ancient state;
Chin: A thousand.
(But the name of the last as shown
on a letter which had been sent to
her from China was:

陳麗仟　Chan Lai Chin
7115-7787-0107

Chan: The Name of an ancient state;
Lai: Beautiful, elegant;
Chin: A thousand.
(This character is written slightly
different from that for 'Chin' in her
other name, but the two are interchangeable.)

Examples of the names of Hakka people

陳氏　Chin See
7115-3044
　　(a woman)

Chin: The name of an ancient state;
See: Woman's maiden name

郭十一　Kwok Seep it
6753-0577-0001

　　(a man)

Kwok: The outer wall of fortifica-
tions; Seep-it: Eleven. (Possibly the
eleventh child in the family.) (The
Hokkiens identify eleven with

110

loneliness, and would not use this
number in a name.)

賴亞九　Lai Ah Kow
6351-0068-0046
　　　(a boy)

Lai: To rely on;
Ah: A familiar name;
Kow: Nine.

劉香　　Lew Heong
0491-7449
　　　(a man)

Lew: a surname only;
Heong: Fragrant.

徐炳勝　Tse Piang Seng
1776-3521-0524
　　　(a woman)

Tse: a surname;
Piang: Bright, luminous;
Seng: Place of scenic beauty.

黃玉　　Wong Yoke
7806-3768
　　　(woman)

Wong: Yellow;
Yoke: A gem, jade.
(This name is very common,
particularly with women)

黃圓　　Wong Yuen
7806-0955
　　　(a man)

Wong: Yellow;
Yuen: Round, circular; (or possibly
complete.)

曾新娣　Chen Sin Tai
2582-2450-1229
　　　(a woman)

Chen: a surname;
Sin: New, recent;
Tai: A younger sister.

高鳳　　Kow Foong
7559-7685
　　　(a woman)

Kow: High, exalted;
Foong: The male phoenix – an
emblem of joy and happiness.
But her name as written on a letter
from China was:

高亞鳳　Kow Ah Foong
7559-0068-7685

(The 'Ah' being merely the familiar
form.)

李約舞　Lee Yok Lin
2621-4766-4729
　　　(a man)

Lee: Plums;
Yok: An agreement;
Lin: A will-o-the-wisp.

黃三　　Wong Sam
7806-0005 (a man)

Wong: Yellow;
Sam: Three

111

Examples of the names of Teochew people

朱大河　Choo Tai Hoe
2612-1129-3109
　　(a man)

Choo: Red;
Tai: Great;
Hoe: A river.

吳二妹　Goh Gee Moey
0702-0059-1188
　　(a woman)

Goh: name of an ancient state;
Gee: Two;
Moey: Younger sister.

(Thus possibly the second daughter in the family.)

許娘妹　Khor Neo Moi
6079-1224-1188
　　(a man)

Khor: A place;
Neo: A girl:
Moi: Younger sister

(Neo and Moi being typically feminine names, even the most shrewd of the malicious spirits should be bedevilled as to this man's sex.)

許名煥　Khor Mia Hwang
6079-0682-3562
　　(a man)

Khor: A place;
Mia: Personal name;
Hwang: Brilliant.

李四　　Lee See
2621-0934
　　(a man)

Lee: Plums;
See: Four; (possibly the fourth son of the family.)

陳武名　Tan Boo Miah
7115-2976-0682
　　(a man)

Tan: The name of an ancient state;
Boo: Military;
Miah: Personal name; (perhaps better 'a renowned warrior').

陳玉土　Tan Gek Thor
7115-3768-0960
　　(a woman)

Tan: The name of an ancient state;
Gek: A gem, jade;
Thor: Earth (one of the five elements.)

(Note: The 'r' in thor is not pronounced; this final 'r' is added by some to words ending in 'o' to indicate that the pronunciation is to rhyme with that of the 'o' in 'rot' rather than the 'o' in 'rote'.)

鄭娘林　Teh Neoh Lim
6774-1224-2651

The: The name of a feudal state;
Neoh: A girl;

(a man)	Lim: A forest.

張加香　Teoh Kar Hiong
1728-0502-7449
　　　(a man)

Teoh: To draw a bow;
Kar: To increase; (it is pronounced 'ka'). Heong: Fragrant.

張亞密　Teoh Ah Beck
1728-0068-5778
　　　(a woman)

Teoh: To draw a bow;
Ah: A familiar name;
Beck: Honey.

鐘豬仔　Teng Too Kia
6988-3727-0098
(an elderly woman)

Teng: A bell;
Too: A pig;
Kia: A diminutive.

(This name Too Kia thus means a piglet; when asked the origin of this unusual name, the old lady was only able to say that it had been given to her by her mother when she was very small.)

陳大目　Tan Thye Mak
7115-1129-4158
　　　(a man)

Tan: The name of an ancient state;
Thye: Big;
Mak: Eyes ('Big eyes Tan').

陳亞妹　Tan Ah Moy
7115-0068-1188
　　　(a man)

Tan: The name of an ancient state;
Ah: Merely a familiar name;
Moy: Younger sister.

(yet another example of a man having a woman's name; When asked about it, he could only say that when he was a few months old his mother called him by this name.)

唐大頭　T'ng Tua Thaw
0781-1129-7333
　　　(an elderly man)

T'ng: The name of a dynasty;
Tua: Big;
Thaw: Head. ('Big-headed T'ng'.)

Examples of the names of Hainanese people

符文洲　Foo Boon Chew
4569-2429-3166
　　　(a man)

Foo: A charm or spell; this name is a very common Hainanese surname, and is rarely used by others.
Boon: Elegant, refined;
Chew: A continent.

(Perhaps it means 'Literary promise as vast as a continent')

符愛玉　Hoo Ai Gaik
4569-1947-3768
　　(a woman)

Hoo: A charm or spell: (it is generally spelt Foo as above).
Ai: Love, affection;
Gaik: A Gem. ('A much-loved jade')

林邢氏　Lim Heng See
2651-6717-3044
　　(a woman)

Lim: A forest;
Heng: The name of an ancient state;
See: Woman's maiden name.

(The last name See always follows immediately after the woman's own surname, which in this case, therefore, is Heng; thus it will be seen that Lim must be the surname of her husband.)

黄亞清　Ooi Ah Seng
7806-0068-3237
　　(a man)

Ooi: Yellow;
Ah: A familiar name;
Seng: Clear, pure.

陳春梅　Tan Choon Mei
7115-2504-2734
　　(a woman)

Tan: The name of an ancient state;
Choon: The spring;
Mei: Plums.
(Really means 'Plum-blossom of the spring').

許世明　Khoo See Min
6079-0013-2494
　　(a man)

Khoo: A place;
See: A generation;
Min: Bright.

(But See is also the first half of the word for 'world', and Beng is the first half of the word 'to understand', so possibly it means 'understanding all things'.)

Examples of the names of Kwongsai people

陳才　Chan Choy
7115-2088
　　(a man)

Chan: The name of an ancient state;
Choy: Talented.

溫文　Wan Mun
3306-2429
　　(a man)

Wan: Mild;
Mun: elegant, refined.

甘氏　Kam Si
3927-3044

Kam: Sweet, pleasant;
Si: Woman's maiden name.

114

(a woman)   (This word Si therefore indicates
                             that the name must refer to a
                             woman, and that the preceding
                             name is her own surname.)

VII   Seals

The seals used by officials and private individuals (but not those formerly used by royalty) are known as 印 Yin. Known since the earliest times, they are still commonly used by Chinese to authenticate documents much as foreigners make use of a signature.[1] The cheaper seals are made from wood or soapstone, or plastic, but more expensive seals may be of metal, or any hard fine-graned stone, or of ivory; the impression is generally made with vermilion red ink.

Three main types of seal may be mentioned, but of these only the first (the Identification Seal) will commonly be found on private letters from Chinese, on certificates and so on:

Identification Seals (名印 Ming Yin)
These must bear the family name (姓 Hsing) and the personal name (名 Ming) of the owner. In addition they may include the following characters:

印	Yin	Seal
之印	Chih Yin	Seal of
章	Chang	Seal
之章	Chih Chang	Seal of

and more rarely the following characters:

| 信 | Hsin | Faith |

---

[1] "Every document, in order to be considered binding or genuine, issuing from a mandarin's establishment, must have his official stamp upon it, not his signature. . . . Mandarins do not sign their proclamations or documents with their names. The stamp makes them official and authentic." (Doolittle, 1868:244.)

117

| 印章 | Yin Chang | Seal |
| 私印 | Ssu Yin | Private seal |

Although the size and shape of these seals varies, the most common are square, with sides of about half an inch. The Hokkiens commonly refer to them as 印 In, and the Cantonese as 圖章 T'o cheung. Examples are given below.

Intimate name Seal (字印 Tzu Yin)
Is used for ornamentation only, not for identification. It may contain the following character in addition to the name:

| 氏 | Shih | Family |

Subject Seal (臣印 Ch'en Yin)
So-called because it could be used by any subject of the emperor. The character by which it is known may be used in place of the surname:

| 臣 | Ch'en | Subject |

The ornamental seals often seen on Chinese paintings or scrolls may not show the surname at all; these ornamental seals are particularly prone to use the specialized ancient seal characters which are sometimes very difficult to decipher.

Identification seals are generally composed in one of these ways:

Second Personal Name	Surname	Chih	Surname	First Personal Name	
Yin	First Personal Name	Yin	Personal Name	Second Personal Name	Surname

Each arrangement can be illustrated with an actual example of a seal (taken from Chinese letters):

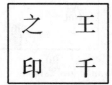

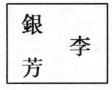

(a)
Yong Yiew Tam — the name of a Foochow man.

(b)
Ong Chien — name of a Hokkien woman. (The character 之 Chih may be inserted where there is only one personal name in order to preserve the symmetry of the seal.)

(c)
Lee Ngan Fong — the name of a Khek woman.

However, seal-makers sometimes depart from the conventional styles, as the following examples show:

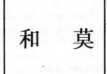

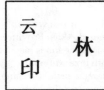

(d)
Mok Woh — a Cantonese woman. Instead of introducing two extra characters 之 and 印 to balance as in (b) above, she has chosen to put her surname and personal name side by side.

(e)
Lim Hoon — a Hokkien woman. She too had only a single character personal name, and she has sacrificed symmetry by introducing the character 印 Yin.

(f)
Chua Pek Khim — a Teochew. This is similar to (a) above, but here the character Chang has been used instead of the more usual character 印 Yin.

119

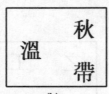

| (g) | (h) | (i) |

Tan Kah Tiong — the name of a district official in Hokkien Province, in the People's Republic. It is similar to (a) and (f) above, but instead of 印 or 章 meaning 'seal' he has employed a star to complete the square.

Wan Thiow Tai — a person from Kwangtung Province. This design is unusual inasmuch as it places the surname (溫) on the left.

Tan How Keng — the seal of a district official in Low Wah, Hokkien Province, affixed to a certificate in May 1957. The characters of his name have been arranged in an unusual order: Top right-hand corner, top left-hand corner, with the word (Seal) in the lower right-hand corner.

(j)

(k)

(l)

Kwek Yik Choo — the name of a Hokkien man. In this oval seal the surname and personal name are inscribed simply from top to bottom, with no additional characters. (The seal is 7/8" high and 1/2" wide.)

Yap Don — a woman from Hokkien Province. This name too is inscribed with no additional characters, the surname above and the personal name below. (It is 1" high and 5/16" wide.)

Ju I — this seal appeared on a letter from Swathow. Neither of these characters is a surname, but in combination they are used as a felicitous greeting meaning 'all as one wishes'. It seems to be used partly as a form of greeting, but no doubt it would also serve in some measure as a form of authentication, since acquaintances would recognize it as being in use by a particular family. (It is 1/2" high and 1/4" wide — much smaller than most seals.)

Note: (i)   The characters 印 Yin and 章 Chang (Seal) can be used as surnames or personal names.

      (ii)   If a Chinese woman has no name-seal of her own, she will sometimes make use of the surname-seal of her husband or son.

In Malaysia at the present time (in 1990s) one does not see name seals used much. But in China it is common to see people proferring their name-seals instead of a signature, for example at banks. The seals are cut to order at small road-side stalls or shops by very skilful craftsmen. (See the Frontispiece)

121

VIII   District Names

These names are called in Chinese 郡名 (*Mand.*: Chün-ming, *Pinyin* Junming, *Hok.*: Kun miaⁿ.)

According to Chinese tradition, persons sharing a common surname are descended from a common ancestor who originated from a particular district of China. Kiang Kang-hu relates that the Chün ming "originated during the Han dynasty (beginning 201 BC). The Empire was then divided into ninety districts or Chün (郡) and all families or clans assigned to one of them where they came from. There are of course many families belonging to one Chün ...".[1] Giles, in the tables appended to his Chinese-English Dictionary[2], gives a list containing ninety district names, and Hauer gives about the same number; both also give the name of the province in China where the district is situated. Tan Pow Tek, on the other hand, lists 125 'Koon Ho' (郡號).[3] One gets the impression that in this matter tradition is more relevant than geographical precision, and that the districts really play a legendary role.

It often happens that two or more surnames have originated in the same district, and so share the same 'district name'; to take one example, one of the 'legendary districts' is 天水 (*Mand.*: T'ien-shui). A list of district surnames which I have gives this as the

---

[1] Kiang Kang-hu, 1934:133.

[2] Giles, pp.1361-63, only two are situated in Hokkien province; Hauer, 1927:77-81, gives the list with only one situated in Hokkien Province.

[3] Tan Pow Tek, 1924:71-87. He refers to the district names as 'Koon Ho' or "Family Titles"; he lists the names alphabetically according to his romanization of the Hokkien pronunciation.

'district name' for twenty-two surnames, including five which are fairly common (see under 'Tien-shui' in Appendix F, under four strokes). Tan Pow Tek (p.85) also lists the twenty-two surnames which originate from T'ien-shui.

But the system is not quite so straightforward, and much field research is needed to establish the precise situation in Malaysia; as we saw in the Introduction, we may be justified in utilizing data on traditional practices in China to build up a somewhat theoretical framework, but this cannot be accepted uncritically as representing the position here. I will give some instances.

Take the case of the well-known Khoo (邱) lineage in Penang. According to Giles (pp.1361,1363) its district name is Ho Nan (*Hok.* Ho Lam) in the province of that name. Similarly, the almanacs and Tan Pow Tek (p.75) consistently give Ho Lam as the district name for the Khoos. They do not mention 新江 Hsin chiang (*Hok.* Sin Kang). We saw above (p.15) that the Khoos regard themselves as originating from Sin Kang village in the Hai Teng district of the Chiangchew prefecture, not far to the west of Amoy.[4] In fact the Khoo lineage in Penang use Sin Kang as their district name, not the "conventional" one of Ho Lam. The Sin Kang name can be seen conspicuously displayed by the neighbouring residents. An office-bearer of the Khoo Clan Association explained to me that membership of the association is not open to every one with the surname Khoo, only to those who trace their origin to Sin Kang Village in the Hai Teng district of the Chiangchew Prefecture, Hokkien Province.

Another instance[5]: It will be seen from Giles (pp.1361,1363), Tan Pow Tek (p.84) and the almanacs that the district name for 謝 (*Mand.* Hsieh, *Hok.* Cheah) is consistently: 陳留 Ch'ên liu, a place situated in Honan Province (see Appendix F, under 'Eleven strokes'). However, the Cheahs in Nanyang use a different district name: 寶樹, Pao Shu M4956 M5879; Yen Ching-hwang[6] notes the

---

[4] For further references, see Franke & Chen, 2, 1985:856.

[5] Dr Newell records that he knew only of the instance just mentioned (Khoo) of one surname being associated with two separate district names (Newell, 1962:70, footnote.)

[6] 1981:89.

use of this district name in Penang; Mr Michael Cheah of Penang confirmed this and gave me these Chinese characters for it; and its use in the Philippines is recorded by See Chinben.[7]

From all this it is evident that persons with any surname linked to a particular district name will feel some affinity with persons having the other surnames originating in the same district, and there are associations which are composed of persons whose different surnames traditionally originated in one district.

Newell, from the anthropological perspective, perceives the surname association (see p.7 above) as a clan, and the total members of all the clans sharing one Chün ming he describes as a phratry.[8]

This brings the question: How exactly does the district name (Chün ming) function in reality?

According to Giles[9] "*Chün Ming* or 'Territorial Appellations' constitute a complimentary form of patronymic, reserved as a rule for use in the documents which pass between two families on the occasion of a marriage. Though occasionally applied to the bridegroom, this is exceptional, and in nine cases out of ten the bride alone is so honoured." Couling puts it more briefly: "The Chün ming 郡名 or territorial appellation is hardly used except for girls on their marriage documents". [10]

This brings us to an important point made by Newell, namely that a man and woman belonging to one phratry, although their surnames may be different, may not marry each other. Thus the need to document and investigate the Chün Ming of the bride-to-be. (Presumably this is checked by the bridegroom's side, on behalf of both sides, to ensure that there is no incompatibility.)

---

[7] See Chinben, 1981:243.

[8] Newell, 1962:68-70; this is mentioned also by Hauer (1926:117); T'ien Ju-K'ang, (1956:21ff) discusses the surname clan fully, but does not mention the district name 'phratry' as functioning in Sarawak.

[9] Giles, 1892:1361.

[10] Couling, S., 1917. *The Encyclopaedia Sinica*. London: OUP p.391.

That may have been the situation in China; in Malaysia the Chün ming has a higher profile. It is often displayed at the front of houses.

Khoo Su Nin recalls that a hundred years ago "the signboard with the words 'Sin Kang' would have been hung above every door of the Khoo clan households, flanked by a pair of verses — one line beginning with 'Sin' and the other with 'Kang'. Today only a handful of façades still retain these signs ..."[11] Until recent years it was very common to see a pair of paper lanterns hanging in front of a Chinese house, white in colour, and with bold characters inscribed on them in red.[12] On one side of each of the lanterns the surname of the occupant of the house would be written; and on the other side the two characters denoting the name of the district in China from which his surname is regarded to have originated.

The lanterns were sometimes suspended so that the surname is to the front on each, and the district name facing inwards towards the house, but it was said to be more correct (and certainly was more usual) to suspend one with the surname to the front and the other with the district name to the front.

At night, on festival occasions, a red candle used to be seen burning in the lantern; usually now it is an electric light that is used to illuminate it. Some families kept the lanterns indoors, bringing them out to public view only on special occasions. During a wedding it used to be usual for the lanterns from the bridegroom's house to be displayed during the wedding procession. These lanterns were favoured particularly by Hokkien people, who called them 字生燈 ('Ji si^n teng'), that is, "Surname lanterns".[13] Nowadays (in the 1990s,) these district name lanterns are not seen so frequently.

---

[11] Khoo Su Nin, *Pulau Pinang* Vol.2, No.1, 1990:26.

[12] Traditionally, lanterns were made of cloth spread over a frame of split bamboo. The upper and lower ends were circular pieces of wood. The lower end was removable, so that the candle could be replaced as necessary; (note from an informant in 1955.)

[13] On this, see "selling the large lantern" on p.73 above.

It will be found more often that the district names will be inscribed on a plaque which is placed in a prominent position over the front door of the house. These plaques are sometimes varnished wooden boards, or they may be boards lacquered black on which the characters are inscribed in gold, or boards painted yellow and inscribed with black characters. A cautionary word here: It is not always easy to distinguish between a board over the door of a private house carrying the district name, and the board bearing the name of the business ('chop') over a shop or shop-house; so far as my experience goes, either of the following will indicate that the plaque is a business-sign, not a district name sign:

Firstly, if the board bears anything other than two large equal sized Chinese characters, then it is a business-sign (business-signs often bear a third character which may be the surname of the proprietor, or the business name itself may consist of three or more characters.)

Secondly, if the board bears a transcription of the name in English writing, again it is a business-sign rather than a district name plaque.

But these indications are not infallible, and an occasional exception may be encountered.

Alternatively, the district name may be painted boldly on a sheet of paper, which is framed and hung over the door like the plaque. And poorer people in rural areas may have to make do with a sheet of red paper, with the district name inscribed in black, pasted over the front of the doorway and exposed to the weather. In a Teochew village in Province Wellesley in the 1950s it was reported that "each villager has the name of his phratry written on red paper over the doorway of his house".[14]

These district name plaques are called in *Mand.* 郡名牌 Chun ming p'ai and in *Hok.* 字姓牌 Ji si^n pai. It should be noted that the characters should always be read from right to left, as you stand facing the house.

---

[14] Newell, 1962:70; as we have seen, he uses "phratry' to denote all those who share one district name.

Occasionally the district names will be used in the place of the surname in the wording of formal invitations sent to the female guests invited to a function; these invitations will be sent out by the lady of the house, who instead of writing her husband's actual surname as part of her name (mentioned on p.40) may write the district name instead; for example, a lady named Yap Sai Hong, the wife of a man surnamed Ong, could (as we have seen) write her name Ong Yap Sai Hong. However, on such formal occasions as that just mentioned, she could substitute the district-name for the surname Ong, and so the invitation would begin (the spelling being in the Hokkien dialect):

歸	平 陽	葉 四 鳳	檢 衽
Kui	Peng Yong	Yap Sai Hong	liam jim
"Woman's maiden name" [15]	*District name for Ong*	*her own name*	*has the honour...*

Apart from its traditional symbolic value, sharing a district name can bring practical benefit. Newell cites an instance where membership of a phratry could bring reduced school fees with it.[16] Our Appendix F, (under 'sixteen strokes',) shows a district name 潁川 Ying-ch'uan (*Hok.* Éng-chhoan), which is in Anhui Province.[17] This is the district name for Tan and seven other surnames, of which two are common in Malaysia as shown: 鍾 C6945, Cheong, and 賴 C6351, Lai. Chong Lee Ngoh[18] records that the Tan Kongsi was the last of the Penang surname clans to maintain its own school. He does not mention the concessions available to pupils of other associated surnames. But I was once told by an official of the Tan Kongsi in Penang that this school, the Ying Chuan Hak Hau, was available to students of any surname,

---

[15] Giles, 1892, No.6419 refers to "... a formula inscribed by women on their visiting-cards, who being forbidden by etiquette to use their husband's name substitute that of their district".

[16] Newell, 1962:140.

[17] See Giles, p.1363. It is illustrated in Figure 5a.

[18] In *Malaysia in History*, 16, No.1, 1973:17.

but those with the surnames Cheong and Lai shared the privilege of those with the surname Tan in getting their fees reduced.

Lin Shan discusses district names, referring to them as clan names, which can be confusing. He states "As a clan name indicates the ancestral home, it is also carved on a man's tombstone to indicate sentiments of his return to the source where he originated".[19] In fact from my observations the place-names which Chinese tombstones usually bear (at the top), are the names of the actual places of origin in China, not the (semi-legendary) district names which we are discussing. As Franke and Chen write "Besides the family name and the personal name tombstones usually give the family's native place (in China) .." Where the district name does occur on a tombstone, (such as 'Sin kang' on that of a member of the Khoo lineage), it seems to me to be an indication that the actual native village is the same as the district name.[20]

Sometimes two strips of white paper will be seen pasted in the form of an 'X' across the district name board placed over the door; this is used as a sign of mourning following a death in the house. Tan Chee-beng records specifically that a strip of paper placed on the lefthand character (looking outwards) denotes that the deceased is a man; one strip on the righthand character (looking outwards) denotes a woman.[21]

Most Chinese almanacs include a list of the Chinese surnames (see Appendix H), giving the appropriate district name for each. Our Appendix F lists the district names for the more common surnames. It should be borne in mind that most of the district names can be linked with other surnames not shown in that list. We have already seen that sources such as Giles and others give lists of the district names.

* * *

---

[19] Lin Shan, 1994:15. He also asserts "A man and a woman of the same clan-name could marry each other, but they could not if they are of the same surname".

[20] See Franke & Chen, 1, 1982:12, 200.

[21] Tan Chee-beng, 1988B:305.

The three components of the name reviewed

If the evidence we have seen has anything to tell us about the theory governing Chinese names, it leads us unquestionably to the conclusion that what binds a Chinese into his present community, what binds him equally to his ancestors and to his descendants without temporal limits, is his surname. The surname is his eternal immovable link with the past and with the future.

In the ideal state his middle name, as a generation name, attaches him to a segment of time within that eternity, to his own lifetime. He will not share it with his ancestors nor with his descendants. Yet it is not his name exclusively as an individual, for he does share it with his brothers and cousins. We observe that in practice the middle name does not often play a paramount role, it can be the least important of his names, and is the name most readily dropped or changed.

When we are informed that up to the Ch'in Dynasty it was the rule to have only one personal name, we may be sure that this had the same function as the third and last element in the name would have nowadays, it was a man's authentic personal name. This marks his individuality. This, always in conjunction with his surname, is his, and his alone, identifying him if not as a member of the wide community, then certainly as a member of his surname clan. This name, in contrast with his middle name, he will not share with his siblings nor his cousins, nor yet (as we have seen) with his ancestors nor his descendants; it is his own individual name.

As for women, sociological theory notwithstanding, we should not too readily accept the postulation that on marriage they pass completely from their own family into that of their husband. From the evidence of the system of naming, we might justifiably conclude that they remain members of their own surname clan until they die.

Appendices

The "Hundred Family Surnames"
百家姓

Arranged in the traditional order

In this list the surnames appear in the same order as they are found in the Chinese published lists which have been studied by generations of Chinese children. They read from left to right, and from top to bottom; each set of four has been numbered in sequence, for ease of reference. The Mandarin romanization is given below each surname. This list is complementary to that given in Appendix B: the numbers given in the third column of Appendix B facilitate finding the corresponding surname in this list; similarly, under each surname in this list has been entered the Chinese Commercial Code number to facilitate finding the corresponding surname in Appendix B; and also the number of the radical of the character to facilitate looking it up in a Chinese dictionary; a guide to the radicals and Chinese commercial code numbers is given in Appendix C.

The two lists in Appendices A and B do not coincide exactly. This list is adapted from a table given in Hauer (1926), comprising 408 single-character surnames and 30 two-character surnames; his spelling has been retained for the Mandarin romanization. It draws also from Weig (1931); Weig gives the same 408 single-character surnames, but appends 77 two-character surnames, as found in some Chinese published lists; I have referred to these occasionally with a number beginning with "D" (for "Doppelnamen").

An asterisk (*) by an entry indicates that a note on it will be found after the list.

408 Single-character Surnames

1 趙 Chao[4] R156 6392	錢 Ts'ien[2] R167 6929	孫 Sun[1] R39 1327	李 Li[3] R75 2621
5 周 Chou[1] R30 0719	吳 Wu[2] R30 0702	鄭 Chêng[4] R163 6774	王 Wang[2] R96 3769
9 馮 Feng[2] R187 7458	陳 Ch'en[2] R170 7115	褚 Ch'u[3] R145 5969	衛 Wei[4] R144 5898
13 蔣 Tsiang[3] R140 5592	沈 Shen[3] R85 3088	韓 Han[2] R178 7281	楊 Yang[2] R75 2799
17 朱 Chu[1] R75 2612	秦 Ts'in[2] R115 4440	尤 Yu[2] R43 1429	許 Hu[3] R149 6079
21 何 Ho[2] R9 0149	呂 Lu[3] R30 0712	施 Shih[1] R70 2457	張 Chang[1] R57 1728
25 孔 k'ung[3] R39 1313	曹 Ts'ao[3] R73 2580	嚴 Yen[2] R30 0917	華 Hua[2] R140 5478

29	金 Kin[1] R167 6855	魏 Wei[4] R194 7614	陶 T'ao[2] R170 7118	姜 Kiang[1] R38 1203
33	戚 Ts'i[5] R62 2058	謝 Sieh[4] R149 6200	鄒 Tsou[1] R163 6760	喻 Yu[4] R30 0827
37	柏 Po[5] R75 2672	水 Shui[3] R85 3055	竇 Tou[4] R116 4535	章 Chang[1] R117 4545
41	雲 Yun[2] R173 7189	蘇 Su[1] R140 5685	潘 P'an[1] R85 3382	葛 Ko[5] R140 5514
45	奚 Hi[2] R37 1153	范 Fan[4] R140 5400	彭 P'eng[2] R59 1756	郎 Lang[2] R163 6745
49	魯 Lu[3] R195 7627	韋 Wei[2] R178 7279	昌 Ch'ang[1] R72 2490	馬 Ma[3] R187 7456
53	苗 Miao[2] R140 5379	鳳 Feng[4] R196 7985	花 Hua[1] R140 5363	方 Fang[1] R70 2455
57	俞 Yu[2] R9 0205, 0358	任 Jen[2] R9 0117	袁 Yuan[2] R145 5913	柳 Liu[3] R75 2692

134

61	酆	鮑	史	唐
	Feng[1]	Pao[4]	Shih[3]	T'ang[2]
	R163	R195	R30	R30
	6785	7637	0670	0781
65	費	廉	岑	薛
	Fei[4]	Lien[2]	Ts'en[2]	Sieh[5]
	R154	R53	R46	R140
	6316	1670	1478	5641
69	雷	賀	倪	湯
	Lei[2]	Ho[4]	Ni[2]	T'ang[1]
	R173	R154	R9	R85
	7191	6320	0242	3282
73	滕	殷	羅	畢
	T'eng[2]	Yin[1]	Lo[2]	Pi[5]
	R85	R79	R122	R102
	3326	3009	5012	3968
77	郝	鄔	安	常
	Ho[5]	Wu[3]	An[1]	Ch'ang[2]
	R163	R163	R40	R50
	9327	6762	1344	1603
81	藥	于	時	傅
	Yo[5]	Yu[2]	Shih[2]	Fu[4]
	R75	R7	R72	R9
	2867	0060	2514	0265
85	皮	卞	齊	康
	P'i[2]	Pien[4]	Ts'i[2]	K'ang[1]
	R107	R25	R210	R53
	4122	0593	7871	1660
89	伍	余	元	卜
	Wu[3]	Yu[2]	Yuan[2]	Pu[5]
	R9	R9	R10	R25
	0124	0151	0337	0592

93	顧	孟	平	黄
	Ku[4]	Meng[4]	P'ing[2]	Huang[2]
	R181	R39	R51	R201
	7357	1322	1627	7806

97	和	穆	蕭	尹
	Ho[2]	Mu[5]	Siao[1]	Yin[3]
	R30	R115	R140	R44
	0735	4476	5618	1438

101	姚	邵	湛	汪
	Yao[2]	Shao[4]	Chan[4]	Wang[1]
	R38	R163	R85	R85
	1202	6730	3277	3076

105	祁	毛	禹	狄
	Ki[2]	Mao[2]	Yu[3]	Ti[5]
	R113	R82	R114	R94
	4359	3029	4416	3695

109	米	貝	明	臧
	Mi[3]	Pei[4]	Ming[2]	Tsang[1]
	R119	R154	R72	R131
	4717	6296	2494	5258

113	計	伏	成	戴
	Ki[4]	Fu[5]	Ch'eng[2]	Tai[4]
	R149	R9	R62	R62
	6060	0126	2052	2071

117	談	宋	茅	龐
	T'an[2]	Sung[4]	Mao[2]	P'ang[2]
	R149	R40	R140	R212
	6151	1345	5403	7894

121	熊	紀	舒	屈
	Hiung[2]	Ki[3]	Shu[1]	K'u[5]
	R86	R120	R135	R44
	3574	4764	5289	1448

125	項	祝	董	梁
	Hiang[4]	Chu[5]	Tung[3]	Liang[2]
	R181	R113	R140	R75
	7309	4376	5516	2733

129	杜	阮	藍	閔
	Tu[4]	Yuan[2]	Lan[2]	Min[3]
	R75	R170	R140	R169
	2629	7086	5663	7036

133	席	季	麻	强
	Si[5]	Ki[4]	Ma[2]	K'iang[2]
	R50	R39	R200	R57
	1598	1323	7802	1730

137	賈	路	婁	危
	Kia[3]	Lu[4]	Lou[2]	Wei[2]
	R154	R157	R38	R26
	6328	6424	1236	0604

141	江	童	顏	郭
	Kiang[1]	T'ung[2]	Yen[2]	Kuo[5]
	R85	R117	R181	R163
	3068	4547	7346	6753

145	梅	盛	林	刁
	Mei[2]	Sheng[4]	Lin[2]	Tiao[1]
	R75	R108	R75	R18
	2734	4141	2651	0431

149	鐘	徐	邱	駱
	Chung[1]	Su[2]	K'iu[1]	Lo[5]
	R167	R60	R163	R187
	6945	1776	6726	7482

153	高	夏	蔡	田
	Kao[1]	Hia[3]	Ts'ai[4]	T'ien[2]
	R189	R35	R140	R102
	7559	1115	5591	3944

157 樊 胡 凌 霍
Fan[2] Hu[2] Ling[4] Ho[5]
R75 R130 R15 R173
2868 5170 0407 7202

161 虞 萬 支 柯
Yu[2] Wan[4] Chih[1] K'o[1]
R141 R140 R65 R75
5713 5502 2388 2688

165 昝 管 盧 莫
Tsan[3] Kuan[3] Lu[2] Mo[5]
R72 R118 R108 R140
2501 4619 4151 5459

169 經 房 裘 繆
King[1] Fang[2] K'iu[2] Miao[4]
R120 R63 R145 R120
4842 2075 5941 4924

173 干 解 應 宋
Kan[1] Hiai[4] Ying[1] Tsung[1]
R51 R148 R61 R40
1626 6043 2019 1350

177 丁 宣 賁 鄧
Ting[1] Suan[1] Fei[2] Teng[4]
R1 R40 R154 R163
0002 1357 6321 6772

181 郁 單 杭 洪
Yu[5] Shan[3] Hang[2] Hung[2]
R163 R30 R75 R85
6735 0830 2635 3163

185 包 諸 左 石
Pao[1] Chu[1] Tso[3] Shih[5]
R20 R149 R48 R112
0545 6175 1563 4258

189	崔	吉	鈕	龔
	Ts'ui[2]	Ki[5]	Niu[3]	Kung[1]
	R46	R30	R167	R212
	1508	0679	6873	7895
193	程	嵇	邢	滑
	Ch'eng[2]	Ki[1]	Hing[2]	Hua[5]
	R115	R46	R163	R85
	4453	1518	6717	3323
197	裴	陸	榮	翁
	P'ei[2]	Lu[5]	Jung[2]	Weng[1]
	R145	R170	R75	R124
	5952	7120	2837	5040
201	荀	羊	於	惠
	Sun[1]	Yang[2]	Yu[1]	Hui[4]
	R140	R123	R70	R61
	5424	5017	2456	1920
205	甄	麴	家	封
	Chen[1]	K'u[5]	Kia[1]	Feng[1]
	R98	R199	R40	R41
	3914	7800	1367	1409
209	芮	羿	儲	靳
	Jui[4]	I[4]	Ch'u[2]	Kin[4]
	R140	R124	R9	R177
	5360	9021	0328	7246
213	汲	邴	糜	松
	Ki[5]	Ping[3]	Mi[2]	Sung[1]
	R85	R163	R119	R75
	3078	6728	4745	2646
217	井	段	富	巫
	Tsing[3]	Tuan[4]	Fu[4]	Wu[2]
	R7	R79	R40	R48
	0064	3008	1381	1566

221	烏	焦	巴	弓
	Wu[1]	Tsiao[1]	Pa[1]	Kung[1]
	R86	R86	R49	R57
	3527	3542	1572	1712
225	牧	隗	山	谷
	Mu[5]	Wei[3]	Shan[1]	Ku[5]
	R93	R170	R46	R150
	3668	7136	1472	6253
229	車	侯	宓	蓬
	Ch'e[1]	Hou[2]	Fu[5]	P'eng[2]
	R159	R9	R40	R140
	6508	0186	1348	5570
233	全	郗	班	仰
	Ts'uan[2]	Ch'ih[1]	Pan[1]	Yang[3]
	R11	R163	R95	R9
	0356	9352	3803	0111
237	秋	仲	伊	宮
	Ts'iu[1]	Chung[4]	I[1]	Kung[1]
	R115	R9	R9	R40
	4428	0112	0122	1362
241	寧	仇	欒	暴
	*Ning[2]	K'iu[2]	Luan[2]	Pao[4]
	R40, R101	R9	R75	R72
	1380, 3942	0092	2940	2552
245	甘	鈄	厲	戎
	Kan[1]	T'ou[3]	Li[4]	Jung[2]
	R99	R167	R27	R62
	3927	9686	0632	2051
249	祖	武	符	劉
	Tsu[3]	Wu[3]	Fu[2]	Liu[2]
	R113	R77	R118	R18
	4371	2976	4569	0491

| 253 | 景 King[3] R72 2529 | 詹 Chan[1] R149 6124 | 束 Shu[5] R75 2631 | 龍 Lung[2] R212 7893 |

| 257 | 葉 Yeh[5] R140 5509 | 幸 Hing[4] R51 1630 | 司 Sse[1] R30 0674 | 韶 Shao[2] R180 7300 |

| 261 | 郜 Kao[4] R163 6750 | 黎 Li[2] R202 7812 | 薊 Ki[4] R140 5636 | 薄 Po[5] R140 5631 |

| 265 | 印 Yin[4] R26 0603 | 宿 Su[5] R40 1372 | 白 Po[5] R106 4101 | 懷 Huai[2] R61 2037 |

| 269 | 蒲 P'u[2] R140 5543 | 邰 T'ai[1] R163 6733 | 從 Ts'ung[1] R60 1783 | 鄂 E[5] R163 6759 |

| 273 | 索 So[5] R120 4792 | 咸 Hien[2] R30 0752 | 籍 Tsi[5] R118 4694 | 賴 Lai[4] R154 6351 |

| 277 | 桌 Cho[5] R24 0587 | 藺 Lin[4] R140 5677 | 屠 T'u[2] R44 1458 | 蒙 Meng[2] R140 5536 |

| 281 | 池 Ch'ih[2] R85 3069 | 喬 K'iao[2] R30 0829 | 陰 Yin[1] R170 7113 | 鬱 Yu[5] R192 7599 |

285	胥 Su[1] R130 5171	能 Nai[2] R130 5174	蒼 Ts'ang[1] R140 5547	雙 Shuang[1] R172 7175
289	聞 Wen[2] R128 5113	莘 Sin[1] R140 5450	党 Tang[3] R10 8096	翟 Ti[5] R124 5049
293	譚 T'an[2] R149 6223	貢 Kung[4] R154 6300	勞 Lao[2] R19 0525	逢 P'ang[2] R162 6646
297	姬 Ki[1] R38 1213	申 Shen[1] R102 3947	扶 Fu[2] R64 2105	堵 Tu[3] R32 1035
301	冉 Jan[3] R13 0373	宰 Tsai[3] R40 1363	酈 Li[5] R163 6786	雍 Yung[4] R172 7167
305	郤 K'i[5] R163 6748	璩 K'u[2] R96 8767	桑 Sang[1] R75 2718	桂 Kuei[4] R75 2710
309	濮 Pu[5] R85 3450	牛 Niu[2] R93 3662	壽 Shou[4] R33 1108	通 T'ung[1] R162 6639
313	邊 Pien[1] R162 6708	扈 Hu[4] R63 2083	燕 Yen[1] R86 3601	冀 Ki[4] R12 0370

317	郟 Kia[5] R163 6751	浦 P'u[3] R85 3184	尚 *Shang[4] R42 0794, 1424	農 Nung[2] R161 6593
321	溫 Wen[1] R85 3306	別 Pieh[5] R18 0446	莊 Chuang[1] R140 5445	晏 Yen[4] R72 2518
325	柴 Ch'ai[2] R75 2693	瞿 K'u[4] R109 4234	閻 Yen[2] R169 7051	充 Ch'ung[1] R10 0339
329	慕 Mu[4] R61 1970	連 Lien[2] R162 6647	茹 Ju[2] R140 5423	習 Si[5] R124 5045
333	宦 Huan[4] R40 1360	艾 Ai[4] R140 5337	魚 Yu[2] R195 7625	容 Jung[2] R40 1369
337	向 Hiang[4] R30 0686	古 Ku[3] R30 0657	易 I[5] R72 2496	慎 Shen[4] R61 1957
341	戈 Ko[1] R62 2047	廖 Liao[4] R53 1675	庾 Yu[3] R53 1662	終 Chung[1] R120 4807
345	暨 Ki[5] R72 2555	居 Ku[1] R44 1446	衡 Heng[2] R144 5899	步 Pu[4] R77 2975

349	都	耿	滿	弘
	Tu[1]	Keng[3]	Man[3]	Hung[2]
	R163	R128	R85	R57
	6757	5105	3341	1738
353	匡	國	文	寇
	K'uang[1]	Kuo[5]	Wen[3]	K'ou[4]
	R22	R31	R67	R40
	0562	0948	2429	1379
357	廣	祿	闕	東
	Kuang[3]	Lu[5]	K'ueh[5]	Tung[1]
	R53	R113	R169	R75
	1684	4389	7067	2639
361	歐	殳	沃	利
	Ou[1]	Shu[2]	Wu[5]	Li[4]
	R76	R79	R85	R18
	2962	3007	3087	0448
365	蔚	越	夔	隆
	Wei[4]	Yueh[5]	K'uei[2]	Lung[2]
	R140	R156	R35	R170
	5588	6390	5688	7127
369	師	鞏	厙	聶
	Shih[1]	Kung[3]	She[4]	Nieh[5]
	R50	R177	R27	R128
	1596	7255	0623	5119
373	晁	勾	敖	融
	Ch'ao[2]	Kou[1]	Ao[2]	Yung[2]
	R72	R20	R66	R142
	2513	0551	2407	5816
377	冷	訾	辛	闞
	Leng[3]	Tze[3]	Sin[1]	K'an[4]
	R15	R149	R160	R169
	0397	6088	6580	7074

381	那	簡	饒	空
	No²	Kien³	Jao²	K'ung¹
	R163	R118	R184	R116
	6719	4675	7437	4500

385	曾	毋	沙	乜
	Tseng¹	Wu⁵	Sha¹	Mieh¹
	R73	R80	R85	R5
	2582	3019	3097	0045

389	養	鞠	須	豐
	Yang³	Ku⁵	Su¹	Feng¹
	R184	R177	R181	R151
	7402	7263	7312	6265

393	巢	關	蒯	相
	Ch'ao²	Kuan¹	K'uai⁴	Siang⁴
	R47	R169	R140	R109
	1560	7070	5566	4161

397	查	後	荆	紅
	Ch'a²	Hou⁴	King¹	Hung²
	R75	R60	R140	R120
	2686	1775	5427	4767

401	游	竺	權	逯
	Yu²	Chu⁵	K'uan²	Lu⁵
	R85	R118	R75	R162
	3266	4555	2938	9310

405	蓋	益	桓	公
	Ko⁵	I⁵	Huan²	Kung¹
	R140	R108	R75	R12
	5556	4135	2719	0361

30 Two-Character Surnames

409 　万　　　俟
Mu⁵　　　k'i²
R1　　　　R9
8001　　　0203

　　司　　　馬
Sse¹　　　ma³
R30　　　R187
0674　　　7456

411 　上　　　官
Shang⁴　　kuan¹
R1　　　　R40
0006　　　1351

　　歐　　　陽
Ou¹　　　yang²
R76　　　R170
2962　　　7122

413 　夏　　　候
Hia³　　　hou²
R35　　　R9
1115　　　0186

　　諸　　　葛
Chu¹　　　ko⁵
R149　　　R140
6175　　　5514

415 　聞　　　人
Wen²　　　jen²
R128　　　R9
5113　　　0086

　　東　　　方
Tung¹　　fang¹
R75　　　R70
2639　　　2455

417 　赫　　　連
Ho⁵　　　lien²
R155　　　R162
6378　　　6647

　　皇　　　甫
Huang²　　fu³
R106　　　R101
4106　　　3940

419 　尉　　　遲
Wei⁵　　　ch'ih²
R41　　　R162
1414　　　6688

　　公　　　羊
Kung¹　　yang²
R12　　　R123
0361　　　5017

421 　澹　　　臺
T'an²　　t'ai²
R85　　　R133
3422　　　5270

　　公　　　冶
Kung¹　　yeh³
R12　　　R15
0361　　　0396

423	宗 政		濮 陽	
	Tsung[1]	cheng[4]	Pu[5]	yang[2]
	R40	R66	R85	R170
	1350	2398	3450	7122

425	淳 于		單 于	
	Shun[2]	yu[2]	Shan[2]	yu[2]
	R85	R7	R30	R7
	8642	0600	0830	0600

427	太 叔		申 屠	
	T'ai[4]	shu[5]	Shen[1]	t'u[2]
	R37	R29	R102	R44
	1132	0647	3947	1458

429	公 孫		仲 孫	
	Kung[1]	sun[1]	Chung[4]	sun[1]
	R12	R39	R9	R39
	0361	1327	0112	1327

431	軒 轅		令 狐	
	Hien[1]	yuan[2]	Ling[4]	hu[2]
	R159	R159	R9	R94
	6513	6562	0109	3698

433	鍾 離		宇 文	
	Chung[1]	li[2]	Yu[3]	wen[2]
	R167	R172	R40	R67
	6945	7180	1342	2429

435	長 孫		慕 容	
	*Chang[3]	sun[1]	Mu[4]	jung[2]
	R57	R39	R61	R40
	7022	1327	1970	1369

437	司 徒		司 空	
	Sse[1]	t'u[2]	Sse[1]	k'ung[1]
	R30	R60	R30	R116
	0674	1778	0674	4500

Notes

No.241. See note by No.1380 in Appendix B (p.165).

No.319. This character (C1424) is found in the published lists of surnames and is given the number 319a by Weig (1931:79). His number 319 corresponds to our C0794, which is the form found elsewhere, e.g. in Giles (1892, p.1359).

No.435 'Chang' - Weig (p.110) compares this with 'Chang' No.24 (C1728).

THE "HUNDRED FAMILY SURNAMES"
Arranged under the Chinese Commercial Code numbers

This is a list of 479 single-character surnames and 40 two-character surnames. It includes all the surnames that are likely to be encountered in Malaysia (and many which may appear only as given names).

The surnames are listed in order of their Chinese Commercial Code numbers, that is according to their radicals, as in most Chinese dictionaries.

Dist. means "Distinguish from" another similar character with which it might be confused.

An asterisk (*) by an entry indicates that a note on it will be found at the end of the list.

The columns contain respectively:

1) The Chinese Commercial Code number.
2) The Chinese character (with short or alternative forms given in parentheses)
3) The number in the traditional "Hundred Family Surnames" list (App. A). Except for numbers between (439) and (503) inclusive which refer to names included in some published Chinese lists but not included in Hauer's list (1926), and are not included in Appendix "A". Numbers beginning with "D." refer to two-character surnames in Weig's list (1931, pp.101-124).
4) The Pinyin romanization
5) The Wade-Giles (Mandarin) romanization, as given in Mathews' Chinese- English dictionary.
6) A common spelling for the name in Hokkien
7) A common spelling for the name in Cantonese

Note Tone marks have been omitted.

Chinese Names

Chinese Commercial Code Number	Chinese Character	Number in Po Chia Hsing	Pinyin Romanization	Wade-Giles Romanization	Hokkien Common Spelling	Cantonese Common Spelling
0002	丁	177	Ding	Ting	Teng	Ting, Tang
0006-1351	上官	411	Shangguan	Shangkuan	Seong-kuan	Siong-koon
0045	乜	388	Nie	Nieh		Mat
0060	于	82, 425, 426 D.29	Yu	Yu	Oo	Ye
0064	井	217	Jing	Ching	Chee	Cheng
0073	亢	(477)	Kang	K'ang	Khong	Hong
0092	仇	242	Qiu	Ch'iu	Kew, Siew	Chou
0109-3698	令狐	432	Linghu	Linghu		
0111	仰	236	Yang	Yang	Geong	Yeong
0112	仲	238	Zhong	Chung	Teong	Choong
0112-1327	仲孫	430	Zhongsun	Chungsun	Teong-soon	Choong-soon
0117	任	58	Ren	Jen	Jim, Lim	Jam, Yam
0122	伊	239	Yi	I	Ee	I
0124	伍	89	Wu	Wu	Goh	Ng
0126	伏	114	Fu	Fu	Hock	Fook
0149	何	21	He	He, Ho	Hoe, Hoh	Ho, Hoo
0151	余	90	Yu	Yu	Oo, Ee	Yu, Yee
0152	佘	(488)	She	She	Seah, Sua	Siah
0157*	佟	D.76	Tong	Tung	Tong	Tung
0186	侯, 夋	230	Hou	Hou	How, Haw	Hou
0205*	俞	57	Yu	Yu	Joo, Loo	Yu
0242	倪	71	Ni	Ni	Geh, Gay	Yi, Nga
0243	倫		Lun	Lun	Loon	Loon
0265	傅	84	Fu	Fu	Poh, Pho	Foo
0300*	僧		Seng	Seng	Cheng	Ch'ng
0328	儲	211	Chu	Chu	Too	Chee
0337	元	91	Yuan	Yuan	Guan	Yoon, Yuen
0339	充	328	Chong	Ch'ung	Chheong	Chung
0350	兗		Yan	Yen	Yean	
0356	全	233	Quan	Ch'uan	Chuan	Choon
0358*	兪	57	Yu	Yu	Joo, Loo	Yu, Ye
0361	公	408	Gong	Kung	Kong	Koong
0361-0396	公冶	422	Gongye	Kungyeh	Kongya	Koongyeh

150

0361-1327	公孫	429	Gongsun	Kungsun	Kongsoon	Koong-soon
0361-5017	公羊	420	Gongyang	Kungyang		
0370	冀	316	Ji	Chi	Kee	Chi
0373	冉	301	Ran	Jan, Ran	Jeam	Yun
0397	冷	377	Leng	Leng	Leng	Lung
0407	凌	159	Ling	Ling	Ling	Leng
0431	刁	148	Diao	Tiao	Teau	Tiew
0441	列		Lie	Lieh	Liat	Lit
0446	別	322	Bie	Pieh	Peat	Pit
0448	利	364	Li	Li	Lee	Li
0491	劉	252	Liu	Liu	Lau, Low	Lau
0525	勞,劳	295	Lao	Lao	Lor	Loo
0545	包	185	Bao	Pao	Pao	Pau
0551	勾	374	Gou	Kou		Kau
0554-1362	北宮		Beigong	Pekung	Pokkeong	Pakkoong
0562	匡	353	Kuang	K'uang	Khong	Khong
0575*	區, 区		Qu, Ou	Ch'u, Ou	Au, Khoo	Khooi, Kow
0587	卓	277	Zhuo	Cho, Chuo	Toh, Tok	Chok
0589-1362	南宮	D.72	Nangong	Nankung	Lam-keong	Namkoong
0592	卜	92	Bu	Pu	Pok	Pok
0593	卞	86	Bian	Pien	Pean	Pian
0603	印	265	Yin	Yin	In	Yian
0604	危	140	Wei	Wei	Hooi	Ngai
0623*	厙	371	She	She		Foo
0632	厲, 厉	247	Li	Li	Lay	Lai
0657	古	338	Gu	Ku	Koh, Kaw	Koo
0670	史	63	Shi	Shih	Soo	She, See
0674	司	259	Si	Szu, Ssu	See, Soo	Shi
0674-1778	司徒	437	Situ	Szu-t'u	Sootoh	Shi-Thoo
0674-4500	司空	438	Sikong	Szukung		
0674-7456	司馬	410	Sima	Szuma	Sooma	Shima
0679	吉	190	Ji	Chi	Keat	Kat
0683	后	D.63	Hou	Hou	Hoh, Haw	How
0686*	向	337	Xiang	Hsiang	Heong	Hiong
0702	吳	6	Wu	Wu	Goh	Ng
0712	呂	22	Lü	Lu	Lu, Loo	Loi, Looi

0719	周	5	Zhou	Chou	Chew, Chu	Chow, Chau
0729-1693	呼延	D.57	Huyan	Hu-yen	Hoh-yen	Foo-yun
0735	和	97	He	Ho, He	Hoe	Woh
0752	咸	274	Xian	Hsien	Huam, Ham	Hum
0761	哈	(494)	Ha	Ha	Har, Gap	Ha
0781	唐	64	Tang	T'ang	Tong	Thong
0794*	商	319	Shang	Shang	Seong	Sheong
0827	喻	36	Yu	Yu	Joo	Yu
0829	喬, 乔	282	Qiao	Ch'iao	Keao	Khiew
0830	單	182	Dan, Shan	Tan, Shan	Tan, Sean	Tan
0830-0060	單于	426	Shanyu	Ch'an-yu	Tan-oo	Tan-ye
0917	嚴, 严	27	Yan	Yen	Giam, Yam	Yim, Gin
0948	國	354	Guo	Kuo	Kok	Kok, Kwok
1016	堂, 坣		Tang	T'ang	Tong	Thong, Hong
1035	堵	300	Du	Tu	Toh	Too
1075	墨	(493)	Mo	Me, Mo	Beck	Mak
1108	壽, 寿	311	Shou	Shou	Sew	Shiow
1115	夏	154	Xia	Hsia	Heah	Hah, Har
1115-0186	夏侯	413	Xiahou	Hsia-hou	Ha-ho	Hah-hou
1132-0647*	太叔	427	Tai-shu	T'ai-shu	Thai-soo	Thai-su
1153	系	45	Xi	Hsi	Hea	Khai
1164	奮, 奋		Fen	Fen	Hoon	Fun
1166-1257	女媧		Nuwa	Nu-wa	Loo-oa	Nooi-wo
1202	姚	101	Yao	Yao	Yau	Yew
1203	姜	32	Jiang	Chiang	Keong	Kiong
1205	姞		Ji	Chi	Keat	Kat
1213	姬	297	Ji	Chi	Kee	Koi
1236	婁, 娄	139	Lou	Lou	Law	Loi
1313	孔	25	Kong	K'ung, K'ong	Khong	Hoong
1322	孟	94	Meng	Meng	Beng	Mang
1323*	季	134	Ji	Chi	Kooi, Kwee	Kwai
1327	孫, 孙	3	Sun	Sun	Sng. Soon	Soon, Sun
1342-2429	宇文	434	Yuwen	Yu-wen	Oo-boon	Yu-man
1344	安	79	An	An	An, Aun	On
1345	宋	118	Song	Sung	Song	Soong

1347	宏		Hong	Hung, Hong	Hong, Heng	Wang
1348	宓	231	Mi	Mi, Fu		
1350	宗	176	Zong	Tsung	Chong	Tsoong
1350-2398	宗政	423	Zongzheng	Tsung-cheng		
1351	官	(411)	Guan	Kuan	Kuan	Koon
1357	宣	178	Xuan	Hsuan	Suan	Soon
1360	宦	333	Huan	Huan	Huan	Huan
1362	宫	240	Gong	Kung	Keong	Koong
1363	宰	302	Zai	Tsai	Chai, Chye	Tsai
1367	家	207	Jia	Chia	Ke, Kah	Ka
1369	容	336	Rong	Yung	Yeong	Yoong, Yong
1372*	宿	266	Su	Su	Sew, Seok	Sook
1379	寇	356	Kou	K'ou	Khaw	Khou
1380*	寧,甯,宁	241	Ning	Ning	Leng, Neng	Leng
1381	富	219	Fu	Fu	Poo, Hoo	Foo
1409	封	208	Feng	Feng	Hong	Foong
1414-6688	尉遲	419	Weichi	Wei-ch'ih	Ut-tee	Wai-chee
1424*	尚	319	Shang	Shang	Seong, Cheong	Siong
1429	尤	19	You	Yu	Yew	Yow
1438	尹	100	Yin	Yin	Oon	Yan, Woon
1446	居	346	Ju	Chu	Koo	Koi
1448	屈	124	Qu	Ch'u	Khoot	Choot
1458	屠	279	Tu	T'u	Toh	Thoo
1471	岳	D.61 (474)	Yue	Yo, Yueh	Gak	Ngak
1472	山	227	Shan	Shan	Suah	San
1478	岑	67	Cen	Ch'en	Gim	Kham, Sam
1508	崔	189	Cui	Ts'ui	Sew	Chooi, Chu
1518	嵇	194	Ji	Chi	Kee	
1560	巢	393	Chao	Ch'ao	Chao	Chou
1563	左	187	Zuo	Tso	Cho	Chor
1563-8003	左丘	D.66	Zuoqiu	Tso-ch'iu	Cho-khew	Chor-yow
1565-3019	巨毋		Juwu	Chu-wu	Koo-boo	Koi-mo
1566	巫	220	Wu	Wu	Boo, Bor	Moo
1572	巴	223	Ba	Pa	Pa	Pa
1580	布		Bu	Pu	Poh	Po

1596	帥, 帅	369	Shuai	Shuai	Soay	Shooi
1598	席	133	Xi	Hsi	Seck	Chik
1601	帶		Dai	Tai	Tua	Tai
1603	常	80	Chang	Ch'ang	Seong	Shiong
1626	干	173	Gan	Kan	Kun	Kon
1627	平	95	Ping	P'ing	Peng	Pheng
1628	年	D.75	Nian	Nien	Lean	Nin
1630	幸	258	Xing	Hsing	Heng	Hung
1655	庫		Ku	K'u	Khor, Khaw	Foo
1660	康	88	Kang	K'ang	Khong	Khong
1662	庚	343	Yu	Yu	Joo	Yu
1670	廉	66	Lian	Lien	Leam	Liem
1675	廖	342	Liao	Liau	Leao	Liew
1684	廣	357	Guang	Kuang	Kong	Kwong
1690*	龐, 庞	120?	Pang	P'ang	Pang, Pung	Phang
1712	弓	224	Gong	Kung	Keong	Koong
1728	張, 张	24	Zhang	Chang	Teong, Teoh	Cheong
1730	強	136	Qiang	Ch'iang	Keong	Khiong
1738	弘	352	Hong	Hung	Hong	Hong
1756	彭	47	Peng	P'eng	Phi, Phee	Phang, Pang
1775	後, 后	398	Hou	Hou	Heo	Hou
1776	徐	150	Xu	Hsu, Su	Su, Chee, Choo	Chui, Choi
1783	從, 从	271	Cong	Ts'ung	Cheong	Choong
1854	恒		Heng	Heng	Heng	Hung, Hang
1920	惠	204	Hui	Hui	Hooi, Kwee	Wai
1947	愛, 爱	D.75	Ai	Ai	Ai, Ay	Oai, Oi
1957	慎	340	Shen	Shen	Seen	San
1970	慕	329	Mu	Mu	Moh, Boo	Mu
1970-1369	慕容	436	Murong	Mu-yung	Moh-yong	Mu-yoong
2019	應, 应	175	Ying	Ying	Eng	Ying
2037	懷	268	Huai	Huai	Huay	Whai
2047	戈	341	Ge	Ko	Koh	Kwor
2051	戎	248	Rong	Jung	Jeong	Jung
2052	成	115	Cheng	Ch'eng	Seng	Seng
2058	戚	33	Qi	Ch'i	Chaik	Chek

154

2071	戴	116	Dai	Tai	Tai, Tay	Tai, Thai
2075	房	170	Fang	Fang	Pung, Pang	Fong
2083	扈	314	Hu	Hu	Haw	Wu
2105	扶	299	Fu	Fu	Hoo	Fu
2388	支	163	Zhi	Chih	Kee, Chee	Chi
2407	敖	375	Ao	Ao, Ngao	Goh, Ngoh	Ngao
2429	文	355	Wen	Wen	Boon	Mun
2455	方	56	Fang	Fang	Png, Hong	Fong
2456	於, 于	203	Yu	Yu	Oo	E
2457	施	23	Shi	Shih	See	Shi
2490	昌	51	Chang	Ch'ang	Cheong	Cheong
2494	明	111	Ming	Ming	Meng, Beng	Meng
2496	易	339	Yi	I	Aik, Ee	Yik
2501	昝	165	Zan	Tsan	Chan	Tsan
2513	晁	373	Chao	Ch'ao	Teao	Siew
2514	時, 时	83	Shi	Shih	See	See
2516	晉, 晋	(458)	Jin	Chin, Tsin	Chin	Chun
2518	晏	324	Yan	Yen	Aun, Wah	On
2529	景	253	Jing	Ching	Keng, King	Keng
2552	暴	244	Bao	Pao		
2555	暨	345	Ji	Chi	Khai	
2580	曹	26	Cao	Ts'ao	Chor	Choo
2582	曾	385	Zeng	Tseng	Chan	Chang
2589	有	D.63	You	Yu	Yew	Yow
2589-3574	有熊		Youxiong	Yu-hsiung	Yew-heong	Yow-yoong
2600	朝		Chao	ch'ao	Teow	Chew
2612	朱	17	Zhu	Chu	Choo	Cheo, Choo
2621	李	4	Li	Li	Lee	Lee, Lei
2629	杜	129	Du	Tu	To, Toh	Thu, toh
2631	束	255	Shu	Shu	Sock	Sok
2635	杭	183	Hang	Hang	Hung	Hong
2639	東, 东	360	Dong	Tung	Tang	Toong, Tong
2639-2455	東方	416	Dongfang	Tung-fang	Tong-hong	Toong-fong
2646	松	216	Song	Sung	Seong	Choong
2651	林	147	Lin	Lin	Lim	Lam, Lum
2672	柏	37	Bo	Pe	Phek, Paik	Phak

155

2686	查	397	Zha	Cha	Char	Char
2688	柯	164	Ke	K'o	Qua, Quah	Kor
2692	柳	60	Liu	Liu	Lew	Liau
2693	柴	325	Chai	Ch'ai	Chye	Chai
2710	桂	308	Gui	Kuei	Kooi, Kwee	Kuai
2718	桑	307	Sang	Sang	Song	Song
2719	桓	407	Huan	Huan	Huan	Hung
2733	梁	128	Liang	Liang	Neo, Neoh	Leong
2734	梅,枚	145	Mei	Mei	Mooi, Boey	Mui
2784*	植		Zhi	Chih	Tit	Chik
2799	楊	16	Yang	Yang	Yeo, Yeoh	Yeong
2806	楚	(459)	Chu	Ch'u	Chor, Chaw	Chho
2837*	榮*,荣	199	Rong	Yung	Eng	Weng
2867	樂	81	Yue	Yueh, Lo	Gak	Lok
2868	樊	157	Fan	Fan	Huan	Fan
2938	權,权	403	Quan	Ch'uan	Kuan	Khun
2940	欒	243	Luan	Luan	Luan	Lun
2953	欽	D.52	Qin	Ch'in	Khim	Kham
2962	歐,欧	361	Ou	Ou	Ou, Ow	Ou
2962-7122	歐陽	412	Ouyang	Ou-yang	Ou-yong	Ou-yeong
2975	步	348	Bu	Pu	Poh	Poo
2976	武	250	Wu	Wu	Boo	Mu
3007	殳	362	Shu	Shu	Soo	Su
3008	段	218	Duan	Tuan	Tuan	Toon
3009	殷	74	Yin	Yin	Oon	Yin
3019	毋	386	Wu	Wu	Boo	Moo
3029	毛	106	Mao	Mao	Moh	Mau, Moo
3055	水	38	Shui	Shui	Swee, Sooi	Sui
3068	江	141	Jiang	Chiang	Kang	Kong
3069	池	281	Chi	Ch'ih	Tee	Tsi
3076	汪	104	Wang	Wang	Ong	Wong
3078	汲	213	Ji	Chi	Kip	Khap
3087	沃	363	Wu	Wu	Ork	Fu
3088	沈	14	Shen	Ch'en, Shen	Sim	Sam, Sum
3097	沙	387	Sha	Sha	Suah, Sa	Sar
3127	法	D50	Fa	Fa	Huat	Fatt

156

3156	洗		Xi	Hsi, Si	Sea	Sei
3163	洪	184	Hong	Hung	Ang, Ng	Hoong
3184	浦	318	Pu	P'u	Phaw	Phoo
3205	涂		Tu	T'u	Thoh	Thu
3266	游	401	You	Yu	Yew, Yu	Yow
3277	湛	103	Zhan	Chan	Sim	Cham
3282	湯	72	Tang	T'ang	Th'ng	Thong
3293	源		Yuan	Yuan	Guan	Yun
3306	溫	321	Wen	Wen	Oon	Wan, Wun
3323	滑	196	Hua	Hua	Kut	Wat
3326	滕	73	Teng	T'eng	Tin	Thang
3341	滿	351	Man	Man	Buan, Muar	Mun
3382	潘	43	Pan	P'an	Phua, Phuah	Phoon, Poon
3422-5270	澹臺	421	Tantai	Tan-tai		
3450	濮	309	Pu	P'u	Phork	Phok
3450-7122	濮陽	424	Puyang	P'u-yang		
3527	烏	221	Wu	Wu	Oh	Woo
3542	焦	222	Jiao	Chiao, Tsiau	Cheow	Chiw
3574	熊	121	Xiong	Hsiung	Him	Yoong
3601	燕	315	Yan	Yen	Eng	Yien
3662	牛	310	Niu	Niu	Goo	Ngow
3664	牟	D.69	Mou	Mou	Boh	Mou
3668	牧	225	Mu	Mu	Bock	Mok
3695	狄	108	Di	Ti	Teck	Tik
3763	玄		xuan	Hsuan	Guan, Hean	Yuen
3769	王	8	Wang	Wang	Ong	Wong
3803	班	235	Ban	Pan	Pun	Pan
3914	甄	205	Zhen	Chen	Chin	Ying, Yan
3927	甘	245	Gan	Kan	Kum	Kam
3942*	甯, 宁, 寧	241	Ning	Ning	Leng, Neng	Leng
3944	田	156	Tian	T'ien	Tean	Thin
3947	申	298	Shen	Shen	Sin	San
3947-1458*	申屠	428	Shentu	Shen-T'u	Sin-toh	San-thu
3968	畢	76	Bi	Pi	Pit	Pat
4101	白	267	Bai, Bo	Pe, Po, Pai	Peh, Pea	Pak

4102*	百		Bai	Pe, Pai	Pah	Pak
4102-6849	百里	D.54	Baili	Pe-li	Peok-lee	Pak-lee
4106-3940	皇甫	418	Huangfu	Huang-fu	Hong-hoo	Wong-pu
4122	皮	85	Pi	P'i	Phoi	Phi
4135	益	406	Yi	I	Aik	Yik
4141	盛	146	Sheng	Sheng	Seng	Seng
4151	盧, 卢	167	Lu	Lu	Loh, Law	Loo
4161	相	396	Xiang	Hsiang, Siang	Seong	Shiong
4234	瞿	326	Qu	Ch'u	Koo	Koi
4258	石	188	Shi	Shih	Cheok, Sek	Siak
4359	祁	105	Qi	Ch'i	Kee	Ki
4371	祖	249	Zu	Tsu	Chaw, Chor	Choo
4376	祝	126	Zhu	Chu	Cheok	Chook
4389	祿	358	Lu	Lu	Lock	Look
4416	禹	107	Yu	Yu	Oo	Yu
4428	秋	237	Qiu	Ch'iu, Ts'iu	Chhew	Chow
4440	秦	18	Qin	Ch'in, Ts'in	Chin	Chan
4453	程	193	Cheng	Ch'eng	Teng, Thieh	Cheng
4472	稽		Ji	Chi	Kee	Khei
4476	穆	98	Mu	Mu	Bock	Muk
4500	空	384	Kong	K'ung	Khong	Hoong
4535	竇	39	Dou	Tou	Toh	Thoo
4545	章	40	Zhang	Chang	Cheong	Chiang
4547	童	142	Tong	T'ung	Tong	Thoong
4555	竺	402	Zhu	Chu	Teok	Yu
4569	符	251	Fu	Fu	Hu, Hoo	Foo
4572	笪	D.74	Da	Ta, Tan	Tan	Than
4619	管	166	Guan	Kuan	Kuan	Koon
4675	簡	382	Jian	Chien	Kun	Kan
4694	籍	275	Ji	Chi, Tsi	Cheap	Chik
4717	米	109	Mi	Mi	Bee	Mai
4745	糜	215	Mi	Mi	Bee	Mi
4764	紀	122	Ji	Chi	Kee	Ki
4767	紅	400	Hong	Hung	Ang	Hoong
4792	索	273	Suo	So	Seck	Sok

4801	紹		Shao	Shao	Seao	Shiu
4807	終	344	Zhong	Chung		
4842	經, 经	169	Jing	Ching	Keng	Keng
4886	練, 练		Lian	Lien	Lean	Lin
4924	繆	172	Miao	Miao	Beo, Bock	Miew
5012	羅, 罗	75	Luo	Lo	Loh, Low	Law, Loh
5017	羊	202	Yang	Yang	Yeoh	Yeong
5040	翁	200	Weng	Weng	Ong, On	Yoong
5045	習	332	Xi	Hsi, Si	Sip	Chap
5049	翟	292	Zhai	Chai	Teck	Tik
5071	老		Lao	Lao	Lau	Loh
5105	耿	350	Geng	Keng	Ken	Khing
5113	聞	289	Wen	Wen	Boon	Men
5113-0086	聞人	415	Wenren	Wen-jen		
5119	聶	372	Nie	Nieh	Leap	Ship, Nip
5170	胡	158	Hu	Hu	Oh, Aw	Woo
5171	胥	285	Xu	Hsu, Su	Soo	Sai
5174	能	286	Neng	Neng	Leng	Nang
5258	臧	112	Zang	Tsang	Chong	Chong
5281	興, 兴, 𦥑		Xing	Hsing	Hin	Heng
5289*	舒	123	Shu	Shu	Soo	Suh
5337	艾	334	Ai	Ai	Gai, Hia	Gnai
5360	芮	209	Rui	Jui	Swee	Joi
5363	花	55	Hua	Hua	Hoay, Huah	Fah
5379	苗	53	Miao	Miao	Beao	Mew
5391	英		Ying	Ying	Eng	Yin
5400	范	46	Fan	Fan	Huan	Fan
5403	茅	119	Mao	Mao	Mou	Mau
5423	茹	331	Ru	Ju	Joo	Ju
5424	荀	201	Xun	Hsun, Sun	Soon	Hsoon
5427	荊	399	Jing	Ching	Keng	Kung
5445	莊, 庄	323	Zhuang	Chuang	Ch'ng, Choong	Chong
5450	莘	290	Shen	Shen	Sin	Sun
5459	莫	168	Mo	Mo	Bock	Mok
5478	華, 华	28	Hua	Hua	Hua	Wah

5502	萬, 万	162	Wan	Wan	Ban	Mun
5509	葉, 叶	257	Ye	Yeh	Yap, Heok	Yip
5514	葛	44	Ge	Ko	Kat, Kut	Kot
5516	董	127	Dong	Tung	Tang	Toong
5536	蒙	280	Meng	Meng, Mung	Mong	Moong
5543	蒲	269	Pu	P'u	Paw, Poh	Phoo
5547	蒼, 苍	287	Cang	Ts'ang	Chong	Chong
5556	蓋, 盖	405	Gai	Kai	Kuah	Koy
5566	蒯	395	Kuai	K'uai	Khuay	Khoy
5570	蓬	232	Peng	P'eng	Phang	Fong
5588	蔚	365	Wei	Wei	Wee	Wai
5591	蔡	155	Cai	Ts'ai	Chua, Chuah	Tsoy, Choi
5592	蔣	13	Jiang	Chiang, Tsiang	Cheow, Cheoh	Chang
5618	蕭, 肖	99	Xiao	Hsiao, Siao	Seow, Siow	Siew, Siu
5631	薄	264	Bo	Po	Pok	Poo
5636	薊	263	Ji	Chi	Kee	Che
5641	薛	68	Xue	Hsueh	See, Shih	Sit, Seet
5661	藏, 茝		Zang	Tsang	Chong	Chong
5663	藍, 兰	131	Lan	Lan	Lam, Lum	Lum, Nam
5677	藺	278	Lin	Lin	Lin	Ling
5685	蘇, 苏	42	Su	Su	Soh, Saw	Su, Soo, Sow
5688	夔	367	Kui	K'uei	Kwee, Kooi	Khui
5713	虞	161	Yu	Yu	Oo	Yu
5816	融	376	Rong	Yung	Yong	Yoong
5898	衛, 卫	12	Wei	Wei	Oay	Wai
5899	衡	347	Heng	Heng	Heng	Hang
5913	袁	59	Yuan	Yuan	Wan, Yuan	Yun
5941	裘	171	Qiu	Ch'iu	Kew	Khau
5952	裴	197	Pei	P'ei	Poay	Fi
5969	褚	11	Chu	C'hu	Thoo	Thu
6007-7024	西門	D.68	Ximen	Hsi-men	Se-boon	Sai-moon
6009	覃		Tan	T'an	Tham	Tam
6034	觀, 观		Guan	Kuan	Kwan	Koon
6043	解	174	Jie	Chieh	Kai	Kai
6060	計	113	Ji	Chi	Keh	Kei

160

6064	訓		Xun	Hsun	Hoon	Fun
6079	許	20	Xu	Hsu	Khor, Khaw	Hoai, Hui
6088	訾	378	Zi	Tzu	Choo	Che
6124	詹	254	Zhan	Chan	Chiam, Cheam	Chim
6151	談	117	Tan	T'an	Tum	Tham
6175	諸	186	Zhu	Chu	Choo, Chee	Choo
6175-5514	諸葛	414	Zhuge	Chu-ko	Choo-kat	Choo-kot
6200	謝	34	Xie	Hsieh, Sieh	Chia, Cheah	Chair, Che
6206	謨		Mo	Mo	Boh	Mo
6222	譙	(495)	Qiao	Ch'iao, Ts'iao	Cheao	Chiew
6223	譚	293	Tan	T'an	Tham	Tam, Hiam
6253	谷	228	Gu	Ku	Kok	Kook
6265	豐, 丰	392	Feng	Feng	Hong	Fong
6296	貝	110	Bei	Pei	Poay	Poi
6300	貢	294	Gong	Kung	Kong	Kong
6316	費	65	Fei	Fei	Hooi, Hwee	Fei
6320	賀	70	He	Ho	Hoe	Hoh
6321	賁	179	Ben	Pen, Fen	Hooi, Pi	Fen
6328	賈	137	Jia	Ku, Chia	Kor	Koo
6351	賴	276	Lai	Lai	Lua, Lye	Lai
6378-6647	赫連	417	Helian	Hŏ-lien		
6390	越	366	Yue	Yueh	Yuat	Yue
6392	趙, 赵	1	Zhao	Chao	Yeo	Chew, Chiu
6424	路	138	Lu	Lu	Law	Loo
6508	車	229	Ju	Chu	Chea	Chair, Kooi
6513-6562	軒轅	431	Xuanyuan	Hsuan-yuan	Hean-Yuan	Hian-yoon
6580	辛	379	Xin	Hsin, Sin	Seng	Sen
6581	辜		Gu	Ku		Ku
6593	農, 农	320	Nong	Nung		
6639	通	312	Tong	T'ung	Thong, Tong	Thong
6646*	逢	296	Feng	Feng	Hong	Fong
6647	連	330	Lian	Lien	Lean	Lin
6708	邊, 边	313	Bian	Pien	Pean	Pin
6717	邢	195	Xing	Hsing	Heng	Ying
6719	那	381	Na	Na	Na	Na

161

6726	邱	151	Qiu	Ch'iu	Khoo, Koo	Yaw, Yau
6728	邴	214	Bing	Ping	Peng	Peng
6730	邵	102	Shao	Shao	Seo	Chew
6733	邰	270	Tai	T'ai	Thye	Thoy
6735	郁	181	Yu	Yu	Heok	Yok
6745	郎	48	Lang	Lang	Long	Long
6748	郤	305	Xi	Hsi	Kheok	Kook
6750	郜	261	Gao	Kao	Koe, Kho	Hou
6751	郏	317	Jia	Chia	Keap	Hip
6753	郭	144	Guo	Kuo	Koay, Kwek	Kok, Kwok
6757	都	349	Du	Tu	Taw	Too
6759	鄂	272	E	O	Gok	Ngow
6760	鄒, 邹	35	Zou	Tsou	Chaw	Soo
6762	鄔	78	Wu	Wu	Aw, Or	Oo
6763	鄉, 乡		Xiang	Hsiang	Heong	Hiong
6769	鄞		Yin	Yin	Goon	Kan
6772	鄧, 邓	180	Deng	Teng	Teng, Theng	Tang, Tung
6774	鄭, 郑	7	Zheng	Cheng	Tay, Teh	Cheng
6782	鄺		Kuang	K'uang	Kong	Khong
6785	鄷	61	Feng	Feng	Hong	Fong
6786	酈	303	Li	Li	Lay	Lai
6847*	釋, 释		Shi	Shih	Sik, Sie	Chak
6855	金	29	Jin	Chin, Kin	Kim	Kam
6873	鈕	191	Niu	Niu	New	Neow
6929	錢, 钱	2	Qian	Ch'ien, Ts'ien	Chee	Chien, Chin
6945	鍾	149	Zhong	Chung	Cheong	Choong
6945-7180	鍾離	433	Zhongli	Chung-li		
6988	鐘, 钟		Zhong	Chung	Cheng	Choong
7022-1327	長孫, 长孙	435	Changsun	Ch'ang-sun	Teong-soon	Chang-soon
7027*	閆	D.50	Yan	Yen	Yam, Geam	Yim
7036	閔	132	Min	Min	Bin	Mun
7051*	閻, 阎	327	Yan	Yen	Yam, Geam	Yim
7067	闕	359	Que	Ch'ueh	Khuat	Chut
7070	關, 関 关	394	Guan	Kuan	Kwan	Kuan

162

Appendix B

7074	闞	380	Kan	K'an	Khum	Kham
7086	阮	130	Ruan	Juan	Gwan	Yoon
7113	陰	283	Yin	Yin	Im	Yem
7115	陳, 陈	10	Chen	Ch'en	Tan	Chan
7118	陶	31	Tao	T'ao	Tor	Tho
7120	陸, 陆	198	Lu	Lu	Liok	Loke
7122	陽, 阳	424	Yang	Yang	Yeong, Yeoh	Yeong, Yong
7127	隆	368	Long	Lung	Leong	Loong
7136	隗	226	Wei	Wei	Wooi, Gooi	Gai
7167	雍	304	Yong	Yung	Yeong	Yong
7175	雙, 双	288	Shuang	Shuang	Seang	Song
7189	雲, 云	41	Yun	Yun	Hoon	Yean, Wan
7191	雷	69	Lei	Lui, Lei	Looi	Loi
7202	霍	160	Huo	Huo, Ho	Hock	Fook
7246	靳	212	Jin	Chin	Kin	Kan
7255	鞏, 巩	370	Gong	Kung	Keong	Hoong
7263	鞠	390	Ju	Chu	Keok	Kook
7279	韋, 韦	50	Wei	Wei	Wee, Ooi	Wai
7281	韓	15	Han	Han	Hun, Han	Hon, On
7300	韶	260	Shao	Shao	Seao	Shiew
7309	項	125	Xiang	Hsiang	Hung	Hong
7312	須	391	Xu	Hsu, Su	Soo	Se
7346	顏	143	Yan	Yen	Gan, Gun	Ngan
7357	顧	93	Gu	Ku	Kaw, Kor	Koo
7402	養	389	Yang	Yang	Yong	Yeong
7437	饒	383	Rao	Jao, Rao	Jeow	Jiu
7456	馬	52	Ma	Ma	Beh, Mah	Ma
7458	馮	9	Feng	Feng	Pang	Foong, Fung
7482	駱	152	Luo	Lo	Loh, Low	Loke
7559	高	153	Gao	Kao	Ko, Koe	Koh, Koo
7599	鬱, 玉	284	Yu	Yu	Oot	Ye
7614	魏	30	Wei	Wei	Gooi	Gai
7625	魚	335	Yu	Yu	Hoo, Hi	Yue
7627	魯	49	Lu	Lu	Law	Loo
7637	鮑	62	Bao	Pao	Pow	Pau
7639-0060	鮮于	D.29	Xianyu	Hsien-yu	Sean-oo	Sin-yu

163

7685	鳳, 凤	54	Feng	Feng	Hong	Foong
7796	麥, 麦		Mai	Me	Bek	Mak, Mark
7800	麴	206	Qu	Ch'u	Kheok	Kook
7802	麻	135	Ma	Ma	Muh, Mua	Mah
7806	黃	96	Huang	Huang	Ooi, Ng	Wong
7812	黎	262	Li	Li	Li, Lay	Lai
7825	黨, 党		Dang	Tang	Tong	Tong
7871	齊, 齐	87	Qi	Ch'i	Cheh	Chai
7893	龍, 龙	256	Long	Lung	Leng, Leong	Loong
7894*	龐	120	Pang	P'ang	Pung	Phang
7895	龔, 龚	192	Gong	Kung	Keng	Khong
8001-0203*	万俟	409	Moqi	Mo-ch'i		
8002*	丌	(441)	Qi	Ch'i, Chi	Kee	Chi
8003	丘	D.66	Qiu	Ch'iu	Khoo	Kiew, Yau
8062	佴	D.70	Er	Erh	Jee	Ee, Ye
8096*	党	291	Dang	Tang		
8112*	冼		Xian	Hsien	Sian	Sin, Sing
8642-0060	淳于	425	Chunyu	Ch'un-yu		
8673	淵, 渊		Yuan	Yuan	Eng, Ean	Yin
8767	璩	306	Qu	Ch'u	Koo	Chok
8895*	禤		Xuan	Hsuan		Huen, Hin
8970	緱	(476)	Gou	Kou	Hou	Hau
9021	羿	210	Yi	I	Geh, Gay	Yi
9252*	夒		Jue	Chueh, Chuoh	Koo	
9310	逯	404	Lu	Lu	Lok	Look
9327	郝	77	Hao	Ho	Hock	Huk
9352	郗	234	Xi	Ch'ih		
9686	鈄	246	Dou	T'ou	Tou	Tau

Notes

0157　Shown in Weig (p.123) as the second part of a two-character surname, but it does exist as a single-character surname too.

0205　This character is interchangeable with 0358.

0300　This is adopted as a surname by Buddhist monks and nuns; cf 6847.

0358　See note by No.0205.

0575 As a surname this is read Ou[1] - see Giles 1892:1389 (1st column).

0623 Dist. 1655.

0686 See p.31, where it is given the spelling in Hokkien of 'A^n'.

0794 See note by No.319 in App. A.

1132-0647 I have also seen a variant 1132-0670 (太史).

1323 Dist. 2621.

1372 Is also pronounced Pinyin 'xiu', Wade-Giles 'Hsiu'.

1380 This character is interchangeable with No.3942 (cf. M4724, M4725).

1424 See note by No.319 in App. A.

1690 See note by 7894 below.

2784 Not found in lists of surnames, but encountered as the name of a Hainanese woman (spelt 'Chek'), and of a Cantonese woman (spelt 'Chik'), confirmed from a name-seal.

2837 Dist. 5391.

3942 See note by No.1380.

3947-1458 I have also seen a variant 3947-1778 (申徒).

4102 See p.31, where it is given the spelling in Hokkien of 'Ah'.

6646 This character has an alternative form — see No.296 in Appendix A (on p.142). cf M1881, M4934.

6847 This is adopted as a surname by Buddhist monks and nuns, especially those who continue to live with their families.

7027, 7051 These characters are interchangeable, cf. M7395. Weig, 1931:116.

7894 is sometimes interchanged (or confused?) with 1690.

8001-0203 万 (8001) is usually pronounced Wan, meaning "ten thousand"; cf. C5502. 俟 (0203) is usually pronounced Szu, and then has the meaning "until, to wait for" (M5595. Weig, 1931:101).

8002 Not found in Mathews' Dictionary; but it is found in *Putonghua — Minnanfangyan cidian*, p.609; confirmation that that form, with two horizontal strokes, is the same as ours (with one) is found in Campbell (1913) pp.313-317.

8096 Cf. No.7825.

8112 Not found in Mathews' Dictionary; but it is to be found in *Putonghua — Minnanfangyan cidian*, p.843.

8895 I have encountered several people with this surname; it is to be found as a surname ('hsüan') in Giles' Radical index (1892, p.1400), and is in *Putonghua — Minnanfangyan cidian*, p.883, as 'xuan'.

9252 This name not confirmed from the dictionaries.

The 214 Radicals, giving the corresponding number for each in the Chinese Commercial Code.

This list is an aid to finding Chinese Commercial Code numbers for names.

It will be seen that many radicals have "overflow" numbers upwards from 8000 representing later additions to the code.

Dist.   means "Distinguish from" another similar character with which it might be confused.

Comp.   means "Compare with" another characters which has similar features.

Abbreviated forms will be found in the place appropriate to the number of strokes in them.

	1 Stroke		23	匚	0571	
1	一	0001, 8001, 9692	24	十	0577	
2	丨	0019, 8011	25	卜	0592	
3	丶	0027	26	卩	0599, 8151	
4	丿	0033, 8026	27	厂	0617, 8118, 8161	
5	乙	0044, 8012, 8031	28	厶	0635	
6	亅	0054	29	又	0642, 8119, 8166	
	2 Strokes		9	亻	0086, 8020, 9687	
7	二	0059, 8015, 8041	18	刂	0430, 8101, 8121	
8	亠	0071	26	卩	0599, 8151	
9	人	0086, 8020, 8045, 9687		**3 Strokes**		
10	儿	0334, 8087, 8096	30	口	0656, 8120, 8167, 9729	
11	入	0354	31	囗	0931, 8188, 8209	
12	八	0360	32	土	0960, 8197, 8216, 9737	
13	冂	0372, 8101	33	士	1102	
14	冖	0382, 8111	34	夂	1111	
15	冫	0391, 8095, 8112	35	夊	1114	
16	几	0415	36	夕	1119	
17	凵	0422	37	大	1129, 8251, 8268	
18	刀	0430, 8101, 8121	38	女	1166, 8261, 8273	
19	力	0500, 8111, 8131	39	子	1311, 8289, 8311	
20	勹	0540, 8116, 8137	40	宀	1336, 8291, 8314 (comp. 116)	
21	匕	0552	41	寸	1407, 8301, 8315	
22	匚	0557	42	小	1420, 8316	

43	尤	1428, 8117, 8152	80	毋	3019	
44	尸	1437, 8311, 8317	81	比	3024, 8632	
45	屮	1469	82	毛	3029, 8633, 8641	
46	山	1471, 8322, 8315, 9710	83	氏	3044	
47	巛	1556	84	气	3049, 8633, 8635	
48	工	1562	85	水	3055, 8659, 8642, 9720	
49	己	1569	86	火	3499, 8696, 8731, 9751	
50	巾	1577, 8341, 8361	87	爪	3629	
51	干	1626	88	父	3637	
52	幺	1633	89	爻	3641	
53	广	1639, 8351, 8369	90	爿	3645	
54	廴	1692 (Dist. from 162)	91	片	3651, 8719, 8778	
55	廾	1699, 8361, 8381	92	牙	3660	
56	弋	1707, 8371, 8382	93	牛	3662, 8721, 8781	
57	弓	1721	94	犬	3689, 8731, 8794	
58	彐	1739	43	尣	1428, 8117, 8152	
59	彡	1747 (compare 190)	61	忄	1800, 8391, 8388	
43	兀	1428, 8152	86	灬	3499, 8696, 9751	
58	彐	1739	87	爫	3629	
60	彳	1761, 8381, 8385	93	牜	3662, 8721, 8781	
61	忄	1800, 8391, 8388	96	王	3768, 8760, 8818, 9713	
64	扌	2087, 8426	113	衤	4355, 8891, 8980 (Dist. fr. 145)	
85	氵	3055, 8642, 9720	122	冗	4986, 9001, 9086	
94	犭	3689, 8731	122	网	4986, 9001, 9086	
140	艹	5335, 9100, 9166	130	月	5131, 9109, 9051 (Dist. fr. 74)	
163	阝	6712, 9321	140	艹	5335, 9100, 9166	
170	阝	7079, 9411	162	辶	6595, 9311, 9374 (Dist. fr. 54)	
		4 Strokes			**5 Strokes**	
61	心	1800, 8391, 8388	95	玄	3763, 8751	
62	戈	2047, 8411, 8414	96	玉	3768, 8760, 8818, 9713	
63	户	2073, 8415, 8421	97	瓜	3900	
64	手	2087, 8418, 8426	98	瓦	3907, 8781, 8850	
65	支	2388	99	甘	3927	
66	攴	2391, 8471, 8489	100	生	3932, 8786, 8856	
67	文	2429	101	用	3938, 8787	
68	斗	2435, 8496	102	田	3944, 8791, 8858	
69	斤	2443, 8491, 8489	103	疋	3988	
70	方	2455, 8499, 8501	104	疒	3994, 8797, 8861	
71	无	2477	105	癶	4096	
72	日	2480, 8501, 8511	106	白	4101, 8821, 8895	
73	曰	2574	107	皮	4122	
74	月	2588, 8524, 8531 (Dist. 130)	108	皿	4129, 8831, 8896	
75	木	2606, 8527, 8541	109	目	4158, 8841, 8898	
76	欠	2944, 8611, 8616	110	矛	4243, 8861, 8925	
77	止	2972	111	矢	4247, 8871, 8926	
78	歹	2983, 8621, 8623	112	石	4258, 8874, 8928, 9694	
79	殳	3007, 8624, 8628	113	示	4355, 8891, 8980	

114	内	4415		150	谷	6253, 9231, 9314
115	禾	4421, 8901, 8986		151	豆	6258
116	穴	4494, 8911, 8999		152	豕	6269, 9241, 9315
117	立	4539, 8921, 9003		153	豸	6282, 9251, 9320
78	歹	2983, 8621		154	貝+	6296, 9254, 9322
80	母	3019		155	赤	6375
85	水	3055, 8642, 8659, 9720		156	走	6382, 9261, 9325
103	疋	3988		157	足	6398, 9268, 9330
109	四	4158, 8841, 8898		158	身	6500
122	⺲	4986, 9001, 9086		159	車	6508, 9291, 9359
145	衤	5902, 9171, 9252 (dist. fr 113)		160	辛	6580, 9301
**6 Strokes**				161	辰	6591
118	竹	4554, 8931, 9006		162	⻎	6595, 9311, 9374
119	米	4717, 8957, 9032		163	邑	6712, 9321, 9386
120	糸	4761, 8970, 9052		164	酉	6788, 9359, 9426
120	糸	4761, 8970, 9052		165	采	6845
121	缶	4970, 8996, 9083		166	里	6849
122	网	4986, 9001, 9086		**8 Strokes**
123	羊	5017, 9011, 9090		167	金	6855, 9367, 9437, 9653
124	羽	5038, 9021, 9095		168	長	7022
125	老	5071		169	門	7024, 9527, 9401
126	而	5079, 9031, 9100		170	阜	7079, 9411, 9532
127	耒	5085, 9101		171	隶	7152
128	耳	5101, 9041, 9105		172	隹	7155, 9421, 9540
129	聿	5124		173	雨	7183, 9431, 9544
130	肉	5131, 9051, 9109		174	青	7230, 9441, 9552
131	臣	5256		175	非	7236
132	自	5261		**9 Strokes**
133	至	5267		176	面	7240
134	臼	5273		177	革	7245, 9451, 9554
135	舌	5286		178	韋	7279, 9461, 9570
136	舛	5292		179	韭	7295
137	舟	5297, 9088, 9152		180	音	7299, 9466, 9573
138	艮	5327		181	頁	7306, 9471, 9575
139	色	5331		182	風	7364, 9481, 9587
140	艸	5335, 9100		183	飛	7378, 9491, 9592
141	虍	5705, 9131, 9213 (Dist. 103)		184	食	7380, 9501, 9594
142	虫	5422, 9141, 9217 (Dist. 182)		185	首	7445
143	血	5877		186	香	7449, 9515, 9611
144	行	5887		**10 Strokes**
145	衣	5902, 9171, 9252		187	馬	7456, 9520, 9613
146	西	6006		188	骨	7539, 9541
118	竹	4554, 8931, 9006		189	高	7559
**7 Strokes**				190	髟	7561, 9551, 9631
147	見	6015		191	鬥	7591
148	角	6037, 9201, 9278		192	鬯	7598
149	言	6056, 9211, 9282		193	鬲	7601

194	鬼	7607, 9561, 9635	204	黹	7832
	11 Strokes		205	黽	7836
195	魚	7625, 9571, 9639	206	鼎	7844
196	鳥	7680, 9601, 9673	207	鼓	7849
197	鹵	7767	208	鼠	7857, 9641, 9696
198	鹿	7773	209	鼻	7865
199	麥	7796, 9621, 9690	210	齊	7871
200	麻	7802	211	齒	7876
	12 + Strokes		212	龍	7893
201	黃	7806	213	龜	7898
202	黍	7810	214	龠	7900, 9652, 9699
203	黑	7815, 9631, 9694			

170

PINYIN INDEX

Pinyin Romanization	Chinese Commercial Code Number	Chinese Character	Number in Po Chia Hsing	Wade-Giles Romanization	Hokkien Common Spelling	Cantonese Common Spelling
Ai	1947	愛, 爱	D.75	Ai	Ai, Ay	Oai, Oi
Ai	5337	艾	334	Ai	Gai, Hia	Gnai
An	1344	安	79	An	An, Aun	On
Ao	2407	敖	375	Ao, Ngao	Goh, Ngoh	Ngao
Ba	1572	巴	223	Pa	Pa	Pa
Bai	4102	百		Pe, Pai	Pah	Pak
Bai, Bo	4101	白	267	Pe, Po, Pai	Peh, Pea	Pak
Baili	4102-6849	百里	D.54	Pe-li	Peok-lee	Pak-lee
Ban	3803	班	235	Pan	Pun	Pan
Bao	0545	包	185	Pao	Pao	Pau
Bao	2552	暴	244	Pao		
Bao	7637	鮑	62	Pao	Pow	Pau
Bei	6296	貝	110	Pei	Poay	Poi
Beigong	0554-1362	北宮		Pekung	Pokkeong	Pakkoong
Ben	6321	賁	179	Pen, Fen	Hooi, Pi	Fen
Bi	3968	畢	76	Pi	Pit	Pat
Bian	0593	卞	86	Pien	Pean	Pian
Bian	6708	邊	313	Pien	Pean	Pin
Bie	0446	別	322	Pieh	Peat	Pit
Bing	6728	邴	214	Ping	Peng	Peng
Bo	2672	柏	37	Pe	Phek, Paik	Phak
Bo	5631	薄	264	Po	Pok	Poo
Bu	0592	卜	92	Pu	Pok	Pok
Bu	1580	布		Pu	Poh	Po
Bu	2975	步	348	Pu	Poh	Poo
Cai	5591	蔡	155	Ts'ai	Chua, Chuah	Tsoy, Choi
Cang	5547	蒼	287	Ts'ang	Chong	Chong
Cao	2580	曹	26	Ts'ao	Chor	Choo

Cen	1478	岑	67	Ch'en	Gim	Kham, Sam
Chai	2693	柴	325	Ch'ai	Chye	Chai
Chang	1603	常	80	Ch'ang	Seong	Shiong
Chang	2490	昌	51	Ch'ang	Cheong	Cheong
Changsun	7022-1327	長孫	435	Ch'angsun	Teongsoon	Changsoon
Chao	1560	巢	393	Ch'ao	Chao	Chou
Chao	2513	晁	373	Ch'ao	Teao	Siew
Chao	2600	朝		Ch'ao	Teow	Chew
Chen	7115	陳	10	Ch'en	Tan	Chan
Cheng	2052	成	115	Ch'eng	Seng	Seng
Cheng	4453	程	193	Ch'eng	Teng, Thieh	Cheng
Chi	3069	池	281	Ch'ih	Tee	Tsi
Chong	0339	充	328	Ch'ung	Chheong	Chung
Chu	0328	儲	211	Chu	Too	Chee
Chu	2806	楚	(459)	Ch'u	Chor, Chaw	Chho
Chu	5969	褚	11	C'hu	Thoo	Thu
Chunyu	8642-0060	淳于	425	Ch'un-yu		
Cong	1783	從	271	Ts'ung	Cheong	Choong
Cui	1508	崔	189	Ts'ui	Sew	Chooi, Chu
Da	4572	笪	D.74	Ta, Tan	Tan	Than
Dai	1601	帶		Tai	Tua	Tai
Dai	2071	戴	116	Tai	Tai, Tay	Tai, Thai
Dan, Shan	0830	單	182	Tan, Shan	Tan, Sean	Tan
Dang	7825	黨		Tang	Tong	Tong
Dang	8096	黨	291	Tang		
Deng	6772	鄧	180	Teng	Teng, Theng	Tang, Tung
Di	3695	狄	108	Ti	Teck	Tik
Diao	0431	刁	148	Tiao	Teau	Tiew
Ding	0002	丁	177	Ting	Teng	Ting, Tang
Dong	2639	東	360	Tung	Tang	Toong, Tong
Dong	5516	董	127	Tung	Tang	Toong
Dongfang	2639-2455	東方	416	Tung-fang	Tong-hong	Toong-fong
Dou	4535	竇	39	Tou	Toh	Thoo
Dou	9686	鈄	246	T'ou	Tou	Tau

172

Du	1035	堵	300	Tu	Toh	Too
Du	2629	杜	129	Tu	To, Toh	Thu, toh
Du	6757	都	349	Tu	Taw	Too
Duan	3008	段	218	Tuan	Tuan	Toon
E	6759	鄂	272	O	Gok	Ngow
Er	8062	佴	D.70	Erh	Jee	Ee, Ye
Fa	3127	法	D50	Fa	Huat	Fatt
Fan	2868	樊	157	Fan	Huan	Fan
Fan	5400	范	46	Fan	Huan	Fan
Fang	2075	房	170	Fang	Pung, Pang	Fong
Fang	2455	方	56	Fang	Png, Hong	Fong
Fei	6316	費	65	Fei	Hooi, Hwee	Fei
Fen	1164	奮		Fen	Hoon	Fun
Feng	1409	封	208	Feng	Hong	Foong
Feng	6265	豐	392	Feng	Hong	Fong
Feng	6646	逢	296	Feng	Hong	Fong
Feng	6785	酆	61	Feng	Hong	Fong
Feng	7458	馮	9	Feng	Pang	Foong, Fung
Feng	7685	鳳	54	Feng	Hong	Foong
Fu	0126	伏	114	Fu	Hock	Fook
Fu	0265	傅	84	Fu	Poh, Pho	Foo
Fu	1381	富	219	Fu	Poo, Hoo	Foo
Fu	2105	扶	299	Fu	Hoo	Fu
Fu	4569	符	251	Fu	Hu, Hoo	Foo
Gai	5556	蓋	405	Kai	Kuah	Koy
Gan	1626	干	173	Kan	Kun	Kon
Gan	3927	甘	245	Kan	Kum	Kam
Gao	6750	郜	261	Kao	Koe, Kho	Hou
Gao	7559	高	153	Kao	Ko, Koe	Koh, Koo
Ge	2047	戈	341	Ko	Koh	Kwor
Ge	5514	葛	44	Ko	Kat, Kut	Kot
Geng	5105	耿	350	Keng	Ken	Khing
Gong	0361	公	408	Kung	Kong	Koong
Gong	1362	宮	240	Kung	Keong	Koong
Gong	1712	弓	224	Kung	Keong	Koong

Gong	6300	貢	294	Kung	Kong	Kong
Gong	7255	鞏	370	Kung	Keong	Hoong
Gong	7895	龔	192	Kung	Keng	Khong
Gongsun	0361-1327	公孫	429	Kungsun	Kong-soon	Koong-soon
Gongyang	0361-5017	公羊	420	Kungyang		
Gongye	0361-0396	公冶	422	Kungyeh	Kongya	Koongyeh
Gou	0551	勾	374	Kou		Kau
Gou	8970	緱	(476)	Kou	Hou	Hau
Gu	0657	古	338	Ku	Koh, Kaw	Koo
Gu	6253	谷	228	Ku	Kok	Kook
Gu	6581	辜		Ku		Ku
Gu	7357	顧	93	Ku	Kaw, Kor	Koo
Guan	1351	官	(411)	Kuan	Kuan	Koon
Guan	4619	管	166	Kuan	Kuan	Koon
Guan	6034	觀		Kuan	Kwan	Koon
Guan	7070	關,关,関	394	Kuan	Kwan	Kuan
Guang	1684	廣	357	Kuang	Kong	Kwong
Gui	2710	桂	308	Kuei	Kooi, Kwee	Kuai
Guo	0948	國	354	Kuo	Kok	Kok, Kwok
Guo	6753	郭	144	Kuo	Koay, Kwek	Kok, Kwok
Ha	0761	哈	(494)	Ha	Har, Gap	Ha
Han	7281	韓	15	Han	Hun, Han	Hon, On
Hang	2635	杭	183	Hang	Hung	Hong
Hao	9327	郝	77	Ho	Hock	Huk
He	0149	何	21	He, Ho	Hoe, Hoh	Ho, Hoo
He	0735	和	97	Ho, He	Hoe	Woh
He	6320	賀	70	Ho	Hoe	Hoh
Helian	6378-6647	赫連	417	Ho-lien		
Heng	1854	恒		Heng	Heng	Hung, Hang
Heng	5899	衡	347	Heng	Heng	Hang
Hong	1347	宏		Hung, Hong	Hong, Heng	Wang
Hong	1738	弘	352	Hung	Hong	Hong
Hong	3163	洪	184	Hung	Ang, Ng	Hoong
Hong	4767	紅	400	Hung	Ang	Hoong

174

Hou	0186	侯,矦	230	Hou	How, Haw	Hou
Hou	0683	后	D.63	Hou	Hoh, Haw	How
Hou	1775	後	398	Hou	Heo	Hou
Hu	2083	扈	314	Hu	Haw	Wu
Hu	5170	胡	158	Hu	Oh, Aw	Woo
Hua	3323	滑	196	Hua	Kut	Wat
Hua	5363	花	55	Hua	Hoay, Huah	Fah
Hua	5478	華	28	Hua	Hua	Wah
Huai	2037	懷	268	Huai	Huay	Whai
Huan	1360	宦	333	Huan	Huan	Huan
Huan	2719	桓	407	Huan	Huan	Hung
Huang	7806	黃	96	Huang	Ooi, Ng	Wong
Huangfu	4106-3940	皇甫	418	Huang-fu	Hong-hoo	Wong-pu
Hui	1920	惠	204	Hui	Hooi, Kwee	Wai
Huo	7202	霍	160	Huo, Ho	Hock	Fook
Huyan	0729-1693	呼延	D.57	Hu-yen	Hoh-yen	Foo-yun
Ji	0370	冀	316	Chi	Kee	Chi
Ji	0679	吉	190	Chi	Keat	Kat
Ji	1205	姞		Chi	Keat	Kat
Ji	1213	姬	297	Chi	Kee	Koi
Ji	1323	季	134	Chi	Kooi, Kwee	Kwai
Ji	1518	嵇	194	Chi	Kee	
Ji	2555	暨	345	Chi	Khai	
Ji	3078	汲	213	Chi	Kip	Khap
Ji	4472	稽		Chi	Kee	Khei
Ji	4694	籍	275	Chi, Tsi	Cheap	Chik
Ji	4764	記	122	Chi	Kee	Ki
Ji	5636	薊	263	Chi	Kee	Che
Ji	6060	計	113	Chi	Keh	Kei
Jia	1367	家	207	Chia	Ke, Kah	Ka
Jia	6328	賈	137	Ku, Chia	Kor	Koo
Jia	6751	郟	317	Chia	Keap	Hip
Jian	4675	簡	382	Chien	Kun	Kan
Jiang	1203	姜	32	Chiang	Keong	Kiong
Jiang	3068	江	141	Chiang	Kang	Kong

175

Jiang	5592	蔣	13	Chiang, Tsiang	Cheow, Cheoh	Chang
Jiao	3542	蕉	222	Chiao, Tsiau	Cheow	Chiw
Jie	6043	解	174	Chieh	Kai	Kai
Jin	2516	晉	(458)	Chin, Tsin	Chin	Chun
Jin	6855	金	29	Chin, Kin	Kim	Kam
Jin	7246	靳	212	Chin	Kin	Kan
Jing	0064	井	217	Ching	Chee	Cheng
Jing	2529	景	253	Ching	Keng, King	Keng
Jing	4842	經	169	Ching	Keng	Keng
Jing	5427	荊	399	Ching	Keng	Kung
Ju	1446	居	346	Chu	Koo	Koi
Ju	6508	車	229	Chu	Chea	Chair, Kooi
Ju	7263	鞠	390	Chu	Keok	Kook
Jue	9252	玃		Chueh, Chuoh	Koo	
Juwu	1565-3019	巨毌		Chu-wu	Koo-boo	Koi-mo
Kan	7074	闞	380	K'an	Khum	Kham
Kang	0073	亢	(477)	K'ang	Khong	Hong
Kang	1660	康	88	K'ang	Khong	Khong
Ke	2688	柯	164	K'o	Qua, Quah	Kor
Kong	1313	孔	25	K'ung, K'ong	Khong	Hoong
Kong	4500	空	384	K'ung	Khong	Hoong
Kou	1379	寇	356	K'ou	Khaw	Khou
Ku	1655	庫		K'u	Khor, Khaw	Foo
Kuai	5566	蒯	395	K'uai	Khuay	Khoy
Kuang	0562	匡	353	K'uang	Khong	Khong
Kuang	6782	鄺		K'uang	Kong	Khong
Kui	5688	夔	367	K'uei	Kwee, Kooi	Khui
Lai	6351	賴	276	Lai	Lua, Lye	Lai
Lan	5663	藍, 芏	131	Lan	Lam, Lum	Lum, Nam
Lang	6745	郎	48	Lang	Long	Long
Lao	0525	勞	295	Lao	Lor	Loo
Lao	5071	老		Lao	Lau	Loh
Lei	7191	雷	69	Lui, Lei	Looi	Loi
Leng	0397	冷	377	Leng	Leng	Lung

Li	0448	利	364	Li	Lee	Li
Li	0632	厲	247	Li	Lay	Lai
Li	2621	李	4	Li	Lee	Lee, Lei
Li	6786	酈	303	Li	Lay	Lai
Li	7812	黎	262	Li	Li, Lay	Lai
Lian	1670	廉	66	Lien	Leam	Liem
Lian	4886	練		Lien	Lean	Lin
Lian	6647	連	330	Lien	Lean	Lin
Liang	2733	梁	128	Liang	Neo, Neoh	Leong
Liao	1675	廖	342	Liau	Leao	Liew
Lie	0441	列		Lieh	Liat	Lit
Lin	2651	林	147	Lin	Lim	Lam, Lum
Lin	5677	藺	278	Lin	Lin	Ling
Ling	0407	凌	159	Ling	Ling	Leng
Linghu	0109-3698	令狐	432	Linghu		
Liu	0491	劉	252	Liu	Lau, Low	Lau
Liu	2692	柳	60	Liu	Lew	Liau
Long	7127	隆	368	Lung	Leong	Loong
Long	7893	龍	256	Lung	Leng, Leong	Loong
Lou	1236	婁	139	Lou	Law	Loi
Lu	0712	呂	22	Lu	Lu, Loo	Loi, Looi
Lu	4151	盧	167	Lu	Loh, Law	Loo
Lu	4389	祿	358	Lu	Lock	Look
Lu	6424	路	138	Lu	Law	Loo
Lu	7120	陸	198	Lu	Liok	Loke
Lu	7627	魯	49	Lu	Law	Loo
Lu	9310	逯	404	Lu	Lok	Look
Luan	2940	欒	243	Luan	Luan	Lun
Lun	0243	倫		Lun	Loon	Loon
Luo	5012	羅	75	Lo	Loh, Low	Law, Loh
Luo	7482	駱	152	Lo	Loh, Low	Loke
Ma	7456	馬	52	Ma	Beh, Mah	Ma
Ma	7802	麻	135	Ma	Muh, Mua	Mah
Mai	7796	麥		Me	Bek	Mak, Mark
Man	3341	滿	351	Man	Buan, Muar	Mun

Mao	3029	毛	106	Mao	Moh	Mau, Moo
Mao	5403	茅	119	Mao	Mou	Mau
Mei	2734	梅	145	Mei	Mooi, Boey	Mui
Meng	1322	孟	94	Meng	Beng	Mang
Meng	5536	蒙	280	Meng, Mung	Mong	Moong
Mi	1348	宓	231	Mi, Fu		
Mi	4717	米	109	Mi	Bee	Mai
Mi	4745	糜	215	Mi	Bee	Mi
Miao	4924	繆	172	Miao	Beo, Bock	Miew
Miao	5379	苗	53	Miao	Beao	Mew
Min	7036	閔	132	Min	Bin	Mun
Ming	2494	明	111	Ming	Meng, Beng	Meng
Mo	1075	墨	(493)	Me, Mo	Beck	Mak
Mo	5459	莫	168	Mo	Bock	Mok
Mo	6206	謨		Mo	Boh	Mo
Moqi	8001-0203	万俟	409	Mo-chi		
Mou	3664	牟	D.69	Mou	Boh	Mou
Mu	1970	慕	329	Mu	Moh, Boo	Mu
Mu	3668	牧	225	Mu	Bock	Mok
Mu	4476	穆	98	Mu	Bock	Muk
Murong	1970-1369	慕容	436	Mu-yung	Moh-yong	Mu-yoong
Na	6719	那	381	Na	Na	Na
Nangong	0589-1362	南宮	D.72	Nankung	Lam-keong	Nam-koong
Neng	5174	能	286	Neng	Leng	Nang
Ni	0242	倪	71	Ni	Geh, Gay	Yi, Nga
Nian	1628	年	D.75	Nien	Leon	Nin
Nie	0045	乜	388	Nieh		Mat
Nie	5119	聶	372	Nieh	Leap	Ship, Nip
Ning	1380	寧甯	241	Ning	Leng, Neng	Leng
Ning	3942	甯	241	Ning	Leng, Neng	Leng
Niu	3662	牛	310	Niu	Goo	Ngow
Niu	6873	鈕	191	Niu	New	Neow
Nong	6593	農	320	Nung		
Nuwa	1166-1257	女媧		Nu-wa	Loo-oa	Nooi-wo
Ou	2962	歐	361	Ou	Ou, Ow	Ou

Ouyang	2962-7122	歐陽	412	Ouyang	Ouyong	Ou-yeong
Pan	3382	潘	43	P'an	Phua, Phuah	Phoon, Poon
Pang	1690	龐	120?	P'ang	Pang, Pung	Phang
Pang	7894	龐, 庞	120	P'ang	Pung	Phang
Pei	5952	裴	197	P'ei	Poay	Fi
Peng	1756	彭	47	P'eng	Phi, Phee	Phang, Pang
Peng	5570	蓬	232	P'eng	Phang	Fong
Pi	4122	皮	85	P'i	Phoi	Phi
Ping	1627	平	95	P'ing	Peng	Pheng
Pu	3184	浦	318	P'u	Phaw	Phoo
Pu	3450	濮	309	P'u	Phork	Phok
Pu	5543	蒲	269	P'u	Paw, Poh	Phoo
Puyang	3450-7122	濮陽	424	P'u-yang		
Qi	2058	戚	33	Ch'i	Chaik	Chek
Qi	4359	祁	105	Ch'i	Kee	Ki
Qi	7871	齊	87	Ch'i	Cheh	Chai
Qi	8002	亓	(441)	Ch'i, Chi	Kee	Chi
Qian	6929	錢	2	Ch'ien, Ts'ien	Chee	Chien, Chin
Qiang	1730	强	136	Ch'iang	Keong	Khiong
Qiao	0829	喬	282	Ch'iao	Keao	Khiew
Qiao	6222	譙	(495)	Ch'iao, Ts'iao	Cheao	Chiew
Qin	2953	欽	D.52	Ch'in	Khim	Kham
Qin	4440	秦	18	Ch'in, Ts'in	Chin	Chan
Qiu	0092	仇	242	Ch'iu	Kew, Siew	Chou
Qiu	4428	秋	237	Ch'iu, Ts'iu	Chhew	Chow
Qiu	5941	裘	171	Ch'iu	Kew	Khau
Qiu	6726	邱	151	Ch'iu	Khoo, Koo	Yaw, Yau
Qiu	8003	丘	D.66	Ch'iu	Khoo	Kiew, Yau
Qu	1448	屈	124	Ch'u	Khoot	Choot
Qu	4234	瞿	326	Ch'u	Koo	Koi
Qu	7800	麴	206	Ch'u	Kheok	Kook
Qu	8767	璩	306	Chu	Koo	Chok
Qu, Ou	0575	區		Ch'u, Ou	Au, Khoo	Khooi, Kow
Quan	0356	全	233	Ch'uan	Chuan	Choon

Quan	2938	權	403	Ch'uan	Kuan	Khun
Que	7067	闕	359	Ch'ueh	Khuat	Chut
Ran	0373	冉	301	Jan, Ran	Jeam	Yun
Rao	7437	饒	383	Jao, Rao	Jeow	Jiu
Ren	0117	任	58	Jen	Jim, Lim	Jam, Yam
Rong	1369	容	336	Yung	Yeong	Yoong, Yong
Rong	2051	戎	248	Jung	Jeong	Jung
Rong	2837	榮	199	Yung	Eng	Weng
Rong	5816	融	376	Yung	Yong	Yoong
Ru	5423	茹	331	Ju	Joo	Ju
Ruan	7086	阮	130	Juan	Gwan	Yoon
Rui	5360	芮	209	Jui	Swee	Joi
Sang	2718	桑	307	Sang	Song	Song
Seng	0300	僧		Seng	Cheng	Ch'ng
Sha	3097	沙	387	Sha	Suah, Sa	Sar
Shan	1472	山	227	Shan	Suah	San
Shang	0794	商	319	Shang	Seong	Sheong
Shang	1424	尚	319	Shang	Seong, Cheong	Siong
Shangguan	0006-1351	上官	411	Shang-kuan	Seong-kuan	Siong-koon
Shanyu	0830-0060	單于	426	Ch'an-yu	Tan-oo	Tan-ye
Shao	4801	紹		Shao	Seao	Shiu
Shao	6730	邵	102	Shao	Seo	Chew
Shao	7300	韶	260	Shao	Seao	Shiew
She	0152	佘	(488)	She	Seah, Sua	Siah
She	0623	厙	371	She		Foo
Shen	1957	慎	340	Shen	Seen	San
Shen	3088	沈	14	Ch'en, shen	Sim	Sam, Sum
Shen	3947	申	298	Shen	Sin	San
Shen	5450	莘	290	Shen	Sin	Sun
Sheng	4141	盛	146	Sheng	Seng	Seng
Shentu	3947-1458	申屠	428	Shen-T'u	Sin-toh	San-thu
Shi	0670	史	63	Shih	Soo	She, See
Shi	2457	施	23	Shih	See	Shi
Shi	2514	時	83	Shih	See	See
Shi	4258	石	188	Shih	Cheok, Sek	Siak

Shi	6847	釋		Shih	Sik, Sie	Chak
Shou	1108	壽	311	Shou	Sew	Shiow
Shu	2631	束	255	Shu	Sock	Sok
Shu	3007	受	362	Shu	Soo	Su
Shu	5289	舒	123	Shu	Soo	Suh
Shuai	1596	帥	369	Shuai	Soay	Shooi
Shuang	7175	雙	288	Shuang	Seang	Song
Shui	3055	水	38	Shui	Swee, Sooi	Sui
Si	0674	司	259	Szu, Ssu	See, Soo	Shi
Sikong	0674-4500	司空	438	Szukung		
Sima	0674-7456	司馬	410	Szuma	Sooma	Shima
Situ	0674-1778	司徒	437	Szu-t'u	Sootoh	Shi-Thoo
Song	1345	宋	118	Sung	Song	Soong
Song	2646	松	216	Sung	Seong	Choong
Su	1372	宿	266	Su	Sew, Seok	Sook
Su	5685	蘇	42	Su	Soh, Saw	Su, Soo, Sow
Sun	1327	孫	3	Sun	Sng. Soon	Soon, Sun
Suo	4792	索	273	So	Seck	Sok
Tai	6733	邰	270	T'ai	Thye	Thoy
Tai-shu	1132-0647	太叔	427	T'ai-shu	Thai-soo	Thai-su
Tan	6009	覃		T'an	Tham	Tam
Tan	6151	談	117	T'an	Tum	Tham
Tan	6223	譚	293	T'an	Tham	Tam, Hiam
Tang	0781	唐	64	T'ang	Tong	Thong
Tang	1016	堂, 坣		T'ang	Tong	Thong, Hong
Tang	3282	湯	72	T'ang	Th'ng	Thong
Tantai	3422-5270	澹臺	421	Tan-tai		
Tao	7118	陶	31	T'ao	Tor	Tho
Teng	3326	滕	73	T'eng	Tin	Thang
Tian	3944	田	156	T'ien	Tean	Thin
Tong	0157	佟	D.76	Tung	Tong	Tung
Tong	4547	童	142	T'ung	Tong	Thoong
Tong	6639	通	312	T'ung	Thong, Tong	Thong
Tu	1458	屠	279	T'u	Toh	Thoo

181

Tu	3205	涂		T'u	Thoh	Thu
Wan	5502	萬	162	Wan	Ban	Mun
Wang	3076	汪	104	Wang	Ong	Wong
Wang	3769	王	8	Wang	Ong	Wong
Wei	0604	危	140	Wei	Hooi	Ngai
Wei	5588	蔚	365	Wei	Wee	Wai
Wei	5898	衛	12	Wei	Oay	Wai
Wei	7136	隗	226	Wei	Wooi, Gooi	Gai
Wei	7279	韋	50	Wei	Wee, Ooi	Wai
Wei	7614	魏	30	Wei	Gooi	Gai
Weichi	1414-6688	尉遲	419	Wei-ch'ih	Ut-tee	Wai-chee
Wen	2429	文	355	Wen	Boon	Mun
Wen	3306	溫	321	Wen	Oon	Wan, Wun
Wen	5113	聞	289	Wen	Boon	Men
Weng	5040	翁	200	Weng	Ong, On	Yoong
Wenren	5113-0086	聞人	415	Wen-jen		
Wu	0124	伍	89	Wu	Goh	Ng
Wu	0702	吳	6	Wu	Goh	Ng
Wu	1566	巫	220	Wu	Boo, Bor	Moo
Wu	2976	武	250	Wu	Boo	Mu
Wu	3019	毋	386	Wu	Boo	Moo
Wu	3087	沃	363	Wu	Ork	Fu
Wu	3527	烏	221	Wu	Oh	Woo
Wu	6762	鄔	78	Wu	Aw, Or	Oo
Xi	1153	系	45	Hsi	Hea	Khai
Xi	1598	席	133	Hsi	Seck	Chik
Xi	3156	洗		Hsi, Si	Sea	Sei
Xi	5045	習	332	Hsi, Si	Sip	Chap
Xi	6748	郤	305	Hsi	Kheok	Kook
Xi	9352	郗	234	Ch'ih		
Xia	1115	夏	154	Hsia	Heah	Hah, Har
Xiahou	1115-0186	夏侯	413	Hsia-hou	Ha-ho	Hah-hou
Xian	0752	咸	274	Hsien	Huam, Ham	Hum
Xian	8112	冼		Hsien	Sian	Sin, Sing
Xiang	0686	向	337	Hsiang	Heong	Hiong

Appendix D

Xiang	4161	相	396	Hsing, Siang	Seong	Shiong
Xiang	6763	鄉		Hsiang	Heong	Hiong
Xiang	7309	項	125	Hsiang	Hung	Hong
Xianyu	7639-0060	鮮于	D.29	Hsien-yu	Sean-oo	Sin-yu
Xiao	5618	蕭	99	Hsiao, Siao	Seow, Siow	Siew, Siu
Xie	6200	謝	34	Hsieh, Sieh	Chia, Cheah	Chair, Che
Ximen	6007-7024	西門	D.68	Hsi-men	Se-boon	Sai-moon
Xin	6580	辛	379	Hsin, Sin	Seng	Sen
Xing	1630	幸	258	Hsing	Heng	Hung
Xing	5281	興,兴,眔		Hsing	Hin	Heng
Xing	6717	邢	195	Hsing	Heng	Ying
Xiong	3574	熊	121	Hsiung	Him	Yoong
Xu	1776	徐	150	Hsu, Su	Su, Chee, Choo	Chui, Choi
Xu	5171	胥	285	Hsu, Su	Soo	Sai
Xu	6079	許	20	Hsu	Khor, Khaw	Hoai, Hui
Xu	7312	須	391	Hsu, Su	Soo	Se
Xuan	1357	宣	178	Hsuan	Suan	Soon
Xuan	3763	玄		Hsuan	Guan, Hean	Yuen
Xuan	8895	褟		Hsuan	Tah	Huen, Hin
Xuanyuan	6513-6562	軒轅	431	Hsuan-yuan	Hean-Yuan	Hian-yoon
Xue	5641	薛	68	Hsueh	See, Shih	Sit, Seet
Xun	5424	荀	201	Hsun, Sun	Soon	Hsoon
Xun	6064	訓		Hsun	Hoon	Fun
Xuan	3763	玄		Hsuan	Guan, Hean	Yuen
Yan	0350	兗		Yen	Yean	
Yan	0917	嚴,严	27	Yen	Giam, Yam	Yim, Gin
Yan	2518	晏	324	Yen	Aun, Wah	On
Yan	3601	燕	315	Yen	Eng	Yien
Yan	7027	閆	D.50	Yen	Yam, Geam	Yim
Yan	7051	閻	327	Yen	Yam, Geam	Yim
Yan	7346	顏	143	Yen	Gan, Gun	Ngan
Yang	0111	仰	236	Yang	Geong	Yeong
Yang	2799	楊	16	Yang	Yeo, Yeoh	Yeong

183

Yang	5017	羊	202	Yang	Yeoh	Yeong
Yang	7122	陽	424	Yang	Yeong, Yeoh	Yeong, Yong
Yang	7402	養	389	Yang	Yong	Yeong
Yao	1202	姚	101	Yao	Yau	Yew
Ye	5509	葉	257	Yeh	Yap, Heok	Yip
Yi	0122	伊	239	I	Ee	I
Yi	2496	易	339	I	Aik, Ee	Yik
Yi	4135	益	406	I	Aik	Yik
Yi	9021	羿	210	I	Geh, Gay	Yi
Yin	0603	印	265	Yin	In	Yian
Yin	1438	尹	100	Yin	Oon	Yan, Woon
Yin	3009	殷	74	Yin	Oon	Yin
Yin	6769	鄞		Yin	Goon	Kan
Yin	7113	陰	283	Yin	Im	Yem
Ying	2019	應	175	Ying	Eng	Ying
Ying	5391	英		Ying	Eng	Yin
Yong	7167	雍	304	Yung	Yeong	Yong
You	1429	尤	19	Yu	Yew	Yow
You	2589	有	D.63	Yu	Yew	Yow
You	3266	游	401	Yu	Yew, Yu	Yow
Youxiong	2589-3574	有熊		Yu-hsiung	Yew-heong	Yow-yoong
Yu	0060	于	82, 425, 426 D.29	Yu	Oo	Ye
Yu	0151	余	90	Yu	Oo, Ee	Yu, Yee
Yu	0205	俞	57	Yu	Joo, Loo	Yu
Yu	0358	兪	57	Yu	Joo, Loo	Yu, Ye
Yu	0827	喻	36	Yu	Joo	Yu
Yu	1662	庾	343	Yu	Joo	Yu
Yu	2456	於	203	Yu	Oo	E
Yu	4416	禹	107	Yu	Oo	Yu
Yu	5713	虞	161	Yu	Oo	Yu
Yu	6735	郁	181	Yu	Heok	Hou
Yu	7599	鬱	284	Yu	Oot	Ye
Yu	7625	魚	335	Yu	Hoo, Hi	Yue
Yuan	0337	元	91	Yuan	Guan	Yoon, Yuen

Yuan	3293	源		Yuan	Guan	Yun
Yuan	5913	袁	59	Yuan	Wan, Yuan	Yun
Yuan	8673	淵		Yuan	Eng, Ean	Yin
Yue	1471	岳	D.61 (474)	Yo, Yueh	Gak	Ngak
Yue	2867	樂	81	Yueh, Lo	Gak	Lok
Yue	6390	越	366	Yueh	Yuat	Yue
Yun	7189	雲	41	Yun	Hoon	Yean, Wan
Yuwen	1342-2429	宇文	434	Yu-wen	Oo-boon	Yu-man
Zai	1363	宰	302	Tsai	Chai, Chye	Tsai
Zan	2501	昝	165	Tsan	Chan	Tsan
Zang	5258	臧	112	Tsang	Chong	Chong
Zang	5661	藏,莊		Tsang	Chong	Chong
Zeng	2582	曾	385	Tseng	Chan	Chang
Zha	2686	查	397	Cha	Char	Char
Zhai	5049	翟	292	Chai	Teck	Tik
Zhan	3277	湛	103	Chan	Sim	Cham
Zhan	6124	詹	254	Chan	Chiam, Cheam	Chim
Zhang	1728	張	24	Chang	Teong, Teoh	Cheong
Zhang	4545	章	40	Chang	Cheong	Chiang
Zhao	6392	趙	1	Chao	Yeo	Chew, Chiu
Zhen	3914	甄	205	Chen	Chin	Ying, Yan
Zheng	6774	鄭	7	Cheng	Tay, Teh	Cheng
Zhi	2388	支	163	Chih	Kee, Chee	Chi
Zhi	2784	植		Chih	Tit	Chik
Zhong	0112	仲	238	Chung	Teong	Choong
Zhong	4807	終	344	Chung		
Zhong	6945	鍾	149	Chung	Cheong	Choong
Zhong	6988	鐘		Chung	Cheng	Choong
Zhongli	6945-7180	鍾離	433	Chung-li		
Zhongsun	0112-1327	仲孫	430	Chungsun	Teong-soon	Choong-soon
Zhou	0719	周	5	Chou	Chew, Chu	Chow, Chau
Zhu	2612	朱	17	Chu	Choo	Cheo, Choo
Zhu	4376	祝	126	Chu	Cheok	Chook

185

Zhu	4555	竺	402	Chu	Teok	Yu
Zhu	6175	諸	186	Chu	Choo, Chee	Choo
Zhuang	5445	莊	323	Chuang	Ch'ng, Choong	Chong
Zhuge	6175-5514	諸葛	414	Chu-ko	Choo-kat	Choo-kot
Zhuo	0587	卓	277	Cho, Chuo	Toh, Tok	Chok
Zi	6088	訾	378	Tzu	Choo	Che
Zong	1350	宗	176	Tsung	Chong	Tsoong
Zongzheng	1350-2398	宗政	423	Tsung-cheng		
Zou	6760	鄒	35	Tsou	Chaw	Soo
Zu	4371	祖	249	Tsu	Chaw, Chor	Choo
Zuo	1563	左	187	Tso	Cho	Chor
Zuoqiu	1563-8003	左丘	D.66	Tso-ch'iu	Cho-Khew	Chor-Yow

Note: Lin Shan (1994:18-20) lists about 350 single-word surnames in alphabetical order of the Pinyin spelling, giving the Chinese character.

Evelyn Lip (1994:110-116) lists about 200 surnames in alphabetical order of the Pinyin spelling, giving the Chinese character, the meaning in English, and the significance in terms of *yin* or *yang*, of the five elements, etc., for choosing auspicious names.

About 265 surnames, arranged according to the number of strokes in the characters, and including abbreviated forms, Chinese commercial code numbers, and common spelling according to the Hokkien pronunciation.

TWO STROKES	3662 Goo 牛	8003 Khoo 丘	1327 Soon 孙	3088 Sim 沈	1350 Chong 宗
0002 Teng 丁	3769 Ong 王	2639 Tang 东	2938 Kuan 权	3695 Teck 狄	1351 Kuan 官
0431 Teau 刁	6772 Teng 邓	4151 Loh 卢	5445 Ch'ng 庄	3763 Hean 玄	1424 Seong 尚
0592 Pok 卜	7175 Seang 双	5663 Lam	5478 Hua 华	4359 Kee 祁	2075 Pang 房
THREE	7189 Hoon 云	7893 Leng 龙	7070 Kwan 关	6508 Chea 車	2490 Cheong 昌
0060 Oo 于	7279 Ooi 韦	**SIX**	**SEVEN**	6580 Sin 辛	2496 Ee 易
1472 Suah 山	7685 Hong 凤	0112 Teong 仲	0149 Hoe 何	6717 Heng 邢	2639 Tang 東
8001 Ban 万	**FIVE**	0117 Jim 任	0151 Oo 余	7086 Guan 阮	2651 Lim 林
5898 Way 卫	0361 Kong 公	0112 Ee 伊	0152 Seah 佘	5618 Seow 肖	2976 Boo 武
FOUR	0545 Pao 包	0124 Goh 伍	0562 Khong 匡	5685 Soh 苏	4500 Khong 空
0064 Chee 井	0657 Kaw 古	0679 Keat 吉	0702 Goh 吳	6760 Chaw	4555 Teok 竺
0337 Guan 元	0670 Soo 史	0683 Haw 后	0712 Loo 吕	7122 Yeoh 阳	5363 Huah 花
0593 Pean 卞	0674 Soo 司	0686 Heong 向	1344 Aun 安	**EIGHT**	6726 Khoo 邱
1313 Khong 孔	1580 Poh 布	2612 Choo 朱	1345 Song 宋	0587 Tok 卓	6728 Peng 邴
1429 Yew 尤	3927 Kam 甘	3068 Kang 江	1478 Gim 岑	0719 Chew 周	6730 Seo 邵
1438 Oon 尹	3944 Tean 田	4102 Pah 百	1566 Boo 巫	0735 Hoe 和	6855 Kim 金
2429 Boon 文	3947 Sin 申	5017 Yeoh 羊	2621 Lee 李	1322 Beng 孟	0917 Giam
2455 Hong 方	4101 Peh 白	5337 Hia 艾	2629 Toh 杜	1323 Kwee 季	1016 Tong
3029 Moh 毛	4258 Cheok 石	0491 Lau 刘	3076 Ong 汪	1347 Heng 宏	1690 Pang 庞

5012 Loh 罗	0186 How 侯	5427 Keng 荆	6753 Koay 郭	5445 Ch'ng 莊	7189 Hoon 雲
6774 Teh 郑	1728 Teoh	6750 Kho 鄒	7115 Tan 陳	5478 Hua 華	7191 Looi 雷
7115 Tan 陈	2837 Eng 荣	7279 Ooi 韋	7120 Liok 陸	6009 Tham 覃	6929 Chee 钱
7120 Liok 陆	2962 Ow 欧	7456 Beh 馬	7796 Bek 麥	6320 Hoe 賀	7685 Hong 鳳
NINE	6392 Teo 赵	7559 Koe 高	7806 Ooi 黃	7118 Tor 陶	FOURTEEN
0752 Ham 咸	TEN	ELEVEN	1380 Leng 寧	7122 Yeoh 陽	0300 Cheng 僧
1471 Gak 岳	0186 How 侯	0948 Kok 國	4886 Lean 练	7309 Hung 項	1380 Leng 寶
2457 See 施	0242 Ge 倪	1016 Tong 堂	TWELVE	7458 Pang 馮	1675 Leao 廖
2646 Seong 松	0407 Ling 凌	1508 Sew 崔	0265 Pho 傅	7051 Yam	1684 Kong 廣
2672 Phek 柏	0781 Tong 唐	1660 Khong 康	0829 Keao 喬	THIRTEEN	2837 Eng 榮
2688 Quah 柯	1115 Heah 夏	2580 Chor 曹	0830 Sean 單	1670 Leam 廉	3341 Buan 滿
3156 Sea 洗	1202 Yau 姚	2733 Neoh 梁	1153 Hea 奚	1728 Teoh 張	3914 Chin 甄
3163 Ang 洪	1203 Keong 姜	2734 Boey 梅	1327 Soon 孫	2799 Yeoh 楊	4619 Kuan 管
4371 Chor 祖	1369 Yong 容	3968 Pit 畢	1381 Hoo 富	2806 Chaw 楚	5049 Teck 翟
4376 Cheok 祝	1776 Chee 徐	4545 Cheong 章	1756 Phee 彭	4389 Lock 祿	5536 Mong 蒙
4416 Oo 禹	2513 Teao 晁	4569 Hoo 符	1920 Hooi 惠	4801 Seao 紹	5543 Paw 蒲
9021 Geh 羿	2514 See 時	4764 Kee 紀	2516 Chin 晉	5502 Ban 萬	6392 Teo 趙
5170 Aw 胡	2516 Chin 晉	4767 Ang 紅	2529 Keng 景	5509 Heok 葉	6769 Goon 鄞
5379 Beow 苗	2692 Lew 柳	5040 Ong 翁	2582 Chan 曾	5514 Kat 葛	6772 Teng 鄧
5391 Eng 英	2693 Chye 柴	5423 Joo 茹	2600 Teow 朝	5516 Tang 董	7136 Gooi 陝
5400 Huan	3184 Phaw 浦	5459 Bock 莫	3266 Yew 游	6124 Cheam 詹	7300 Seao 邵
5403 Mou 茅	3205 Thoh 涂	5913 Yuan 袁	3282 Th'ng 湯	6328 Kor 賈	7402 Yong 養
6733 Thye 部	4440 Chin 秦	6079 Khaw 許	3306 Oon 溫	6759 Gok 鄂	FIFTEEN
6735 Heok 郁	5105 Ken 耿	6647 Lean 連	4453 Teng 程	6762 Aw 鄒	0632 Lay 厲

188

1075 Beck 墨	7167 Yong 雍	7202 Hok 霍	6945 Cheong 鍾	5677 Lin 藺	2938 Kuan 權
1070 Moh 莫	7627 Law 魯	7482 Loh 駱	7893 Leng 龍	6223 Tham 譚	TWENTY-THREE
2868 Huan 樊	7812 Lay 黎	7637 Pow 鮑	EIGHTEEN	TWENTY	6786 Lay 酈
3382 Phuah 潘	SIXTEEN	SEVENTEEN	4234 Koo 瞿	1690 Pang 龐	7070 Kwan 關
3574 Him 熊	0491 Lau 劉	2071 Tai 戴	5119 Leap 聶	5685 Saw 蘇	7895 Keng 襲
4472 Kee 稽	2962 Ou 歐	4675 Kan 簡	7175 Seang 雙	6487 Sik 釋	TWENTY-FIVE
5591 Chuah 蔡	4151 Loh 盧	4886 Lean 練	7281 Han 韓	7614 Gooi 魏	6034 Kuan 觀
6151 Tum 談	4476 Bock 穆	8970 Hou 緱	7346 Gan 顏	TWENTY-ONE	
6175 Choo 諸	5592 Cheoh 將	5636 Kee 薊	NINETEEN	5012 Loh 羅	
6760 Chaw 鄒	5899 Heng 衡	5641 See 薛	0917 Giam 嚴	7357 Kor 顧	
6774 Teh 鄭	6351 Lua 賴	6200 Cheah 謝	5618 Seow 蕭	7437 Jeow 饒	
7051 Yam 閆	6929 Chee 錢	6782 Kong 鄺	5663 Lam 藍	TWENTY-TWO	

A List of the common District names, showing the surnames they most usually denote

This table shows the District names for the main surnames used in Malaysia. The first character of each District name is on the right, and the second is to its left, as they appear on the District name board over the doorway. The number of the character in Mathews' dictionary is given. The District names are arranged according to the number of strokes in the first character of the District name. Thus even with a modest knowledge of Chinese characters it is possible to identify a District name, and therefore to surmise the possible surname of the occupant. The common spelling of the surnames is given in the Hokkien dialect, together with the Chinese Commercial Code number. Illustrations of District name boards are given in Figure 5. Sometimes the District name is found inscribed on one side of a lantern hung before the house; where this is found, the actual surname usually appears on a matching lantern alongside it (see p.126).

If you wish to find the district name linked to a particular surname, refer to one of the published "Hundred Family Surnames" lists described on p.4.

An asterisk (*) by an entry refers the reader to the notes after the list.

'C' = Chinese Commercial Code number
'M' = Mathews' Chinese-English Dictionary
'G' = Giles' Chinese-English Dictionary.

THREE STROKES

Shang-tang 黨上
M5669 M6095

馮 Pang   C7458

Hsia-p'ei   邳下
M2520 G8827

余 Oo   C0151

FOUR STROKES

T'ien-shui 水天
M6361 M5922

趙 Teo   C6392

秦 Chin   C4440

嚴 Geam   C0917

尹 Oon   C1438

莊 Ch'ng   C5445

T'ai-yüan 原太
M6020 M7725

王 Ong   C3769

祝 Chiok   C4376

郭 Kwek   C6753

霍 Hok   C7202

Nei-huang 黄內
M4766 M2297

駱 Loh   C7482

Chung-shan 山中
M1504 M5630

甄 Chin   C3914

FIVE STROKES

Hung-nung 農弘
M2380 M4768

楊 Yeoh   C2799

談 Tam   C6151

P'ing-yang 陽平
M5303 M7265

汪 Ong   C3076

巫 Boo   C1566

SIX STROKES

An-ting 定安
M26 M6393

伍 Goh   C0124

梁 Neoh   C2733

胡 Aw   C5170

蒙 Mong   C5536

程 Teng   C4453

Ju-nan   南汝
M3142 M4620

周 Chew   C0719

藍 Lam   C5663

Chiang-hsia 夏江
M638 M2521

黃 Ng, Wee   C7806

Hsi-ho   河西
M2460 M2111

林 Lim   C2651

毛 Moh   C3029

SEVEN STROKES

Wu-hsing   興吳
M7201 M2753

沈 Sim   C3088

尤 Yew   C1429

施 See   C2457

姚 Yau   C1202

Fu-fêng   風扶
M1909 M1890

馬 Beh   C7456

P'ei-kuo   國沛
M5020 M3738

朱 Choo   C2612

EIGHT STROKES

Yen-ling   延陵
M7342 M4067

吳 Goh   C0702

Ho-tung   東河
M2111 M6605

呂 Loo   C0712

薛 Sih   C5641

Ho-nan   南河
M2111 M4260

方 Png　　C2455
穆 Bok　　C4476
蕭 Seow　　C5618
邱 Khoo　　C6726
Wu-ling　　陵武
M7195 4067
蘇 Saw　　C5685
顧 Kaw　　C7357
龔 Keng　　C7895
Ching-chao 兆京
M1127 M247
宋 Song　　C1345
杜 Toh　　C2629
黎 Lei　　C7812
Tung-hai　　海東
M6605 M2014
徐 Chee　　C1776
Ho-nei　　內河
M2111 M4766
陸 Liok　　C7120
司 See　　C0674
Ho-chien　　間河
M2111 M835
凌 Leng　　C0407
詹 Chiam　　C6124

NINE STROKES
Nan-yang　　陽南
M4260 M7265
韓 Han　　C7281
岑 Gim　　C1478
鄧 Teng　　C6772
葉 Yap　　C5509

Figure 5: District name boards
Such boards are displayed over the front doors of many traditional houses. These three boards are:

5a. The District name 'Ying-ch'uan' (Éng Chhoan), for the surname 'Tan' – it was seen near the Tan Kongsi, off Beach Street, Penang. See p.199 (16 strokes); also see text p.128.

5b. The District name 'Lung-hsi' – see p.200 (19 strokes); also p.205 (number 4). It was outside a house occupied by a 'Lee' family.

5c. The District name 'Hsin-chiang' – see p.198 (13 strokes); also text p.129. This board was situated in Cannon Square, Penang, and marked a house occupied by a 'Khoo' family. Unlike many district names, this can be identified quite definitely with the place of origin in China. As such, it may appear on tombstones as the district of origin of the deceased. For its occurrence on a stone from Pulau Langkawi, Kedah, dated 1920 and commemorating a Khoo, see e.g. Franke & Chen (1, 1982:200).

TEN STROKES

Fan-yang　陽范
M1778 M7265

盧 Law　C4151

Kao-yang　陽高
M3290 M7265

許 Khaw　C6079

Kao-p'ing　平高
M3290 M5303

范 Huan　C5400

Chin-yang　陽晉
M1088 M7265

唐 Tong　C0781

ELEVEN STROKES

Ch'ên-liu　留陳
M339 M4083

謝 Cheah　C6200
阮 Ng　　C7086
伊 Ee　　C0122

Ch'ing-ho　河清
M1171 M2111

張 Teoh　C1728
傅 Poh　C0265
溫 Oon*　C3306

TWELVE STROKES

P'êng-ch'êng　城彭
M5060 M380

錢 Chee　C6929

Fêng-yi　翊馮
M1895 M3047

雷 Looi　C7191
白 Peh*　C4101

Po-ling　陵博
M5322 M4067

邵 Seo　C6730

Figure 6: Almanacs

A specimen page from the list of surnames (including District names) given in an almanac published in Hong Kong for the year 1991-92. See Appendix H, esp. p.205.

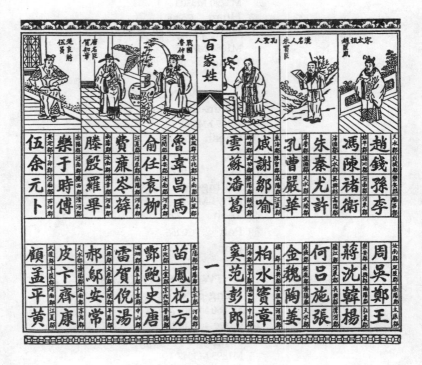

Kuei-chi* 稽會
M2345 M427

夏 Heah C1115

Yen-mên 門雁
M7404 M4418

田 Tean C3944

P'o-hai 海渤
G9426 M2014

高 Ko C7559

甘 Kam C3927

THIRTEEN STROKES

Chü-lu 鹿鉅
M1554 M4203

魏 Gooi C7614

莫 Bock C5459

Hsin-an 安新
M2737 M26

古 Kaw C0657

Hsin-chiang* 江新
M2737 M638

邱 Khoo C6726

FOURTEEN STROKES

Yung-yang 陽滎
M7582* M7265

鄭 Tay C6774

潘 Phua C3382

Kuang-p'ing 平廣
M3590 M5303

賀 Ho C6320

Ch'i-chün 郡齊
M560 M1718

譚 Tham* C6223

FIFTEEN STROKES

Lo-an 安樂
M4129 M26

197

Chinese Names

孫 Soon   C1327
蔣 Cheo   C5592
    Lu-kuo   國魯
    M4176 M3738
孔 Khong   C1313
顏 Gan   C7346
曾 Chan   C2582

SIXTEEN STROKES
Ying-ch'uan 川穎
M7485 M1439
陳 Tan   C7115
鍾 Cheong   C6945
賴 Lai   C6351
    Yü-chang   章豫
    M7603 M182
羅 Low   C5012
    Tun-huang   煌燉
    M6575 M2290
洪 Ang   C3163

SEVENTEEN STROKES
Chi-yang   陽濟
M459 M7265
陶 To   C7118
江 Kang   C3068
蔡 Chuah   C5591
柯 Quah   C2688
丁 Teng   C0002

NINETEEN STROKES
Lung-hsi   西隴
M4276 M2460
李 Lee   C2621
彭 Phee   C1756
董 Tang   C5516

Lü-chang　江盧
M4158 M638

何　Ho　　C0149

Ch'iao-kuo　國譙
M758 M3738

曹　Cho　　C2580

戴　Tay　　C2071

TWENTY STROKES

Pao-shu*　樹實
M4956 M5879

謝　Cheah　C6200

TWENTY FOUR STROKES

Yen-kuan　官鹽
M7352 M3552

翁　Ong　　C5040

Notes to the table

In some cases where the 2nd element of the District name is given as 'kuo' (M3738), Tan Pow Tek (pp.71-87) gives instead 'chün' (M1718).

*Oon C3306: Tan Pow Tek (p.81) gives this under the District name 'P'ing-yüan' M5303 M7725; Giles (1362-3) gives it under the District name 'T'ai-yüan'.

*Peh C4101: Giles (p.1363) gives as the District name 'Nan-yang'; so does Tan Pow Tek (p.78).

*Yung-yang: Many lists show M7586 榮 in place of M7582.

*Tham C6223: Giles (1362-3) gives it under the District name 'P'ing-yin'.

*Kuei-chi: Tan Pow Tek (p.75) gives the characters for Kuei-chi 會稽 (M2345 M426). For pronunciation Kuei, see G6466.

*Hsin-chiang　) These two have been encountered, but I have
*Pao-shu　　　) not found them in the lists of District Names.

Some western names commonly used by Chinese, with usual Chinese transliterations.

English	C.C.C.Nos.	Chinese	Mandarin	Hokkien
Aaron	0068-0243	亞倫	Ya-lun	A-lun
Adam	0068-3981	亞當	Ya-tang	A-tong
Anna	1344-1226	安娜	An-no	An-na
Anna	0068-2169	亞拿	Ya-na	A-na
Antony	1344-1122-1441	安多尼	An-to-ni	An-to-ni
Charlie	2686-3810	查理	Ch'a-li	Cha-li
Daisy	5530-4828	蒂絲	Ti-szu	Te-si
David	1129-5898	大衛	Ta-wei	Tai-oe
David	1129-7075	大辟	Ta-pi	Tai-pit
Dolly	1122-5461	多莉	To-li	To-li
Eve	1115-1216	夏娃	Hsia-wa	Ha-oa
Fifi	7378-7378	飛飛	Fei-fei	Hui-hui
Helen	1115-3781	夏玲	Hsia-ling	He-leng
Irene	1947-5571	愛蓮	Ai-lien	Ai-lian
Ivy	1947-1979	愛慧	Ai-hui	Ai-hui
Job	4766-0130	約伯	Yo-pe	Iok-pek
Jacob	7161-0677	雅各	Ya-ko	Nga-kok
Joseph	4766-3844	約瑟	Yo-se	Iok-Sek
John	4766-5060	約翰	Yo-han	Iok-han
Lilian	7787-5571	麗蓮	Li-lien	Le-lian
Lily	5461-5461	莉莉	Li-li	Li-li
Lily	7787-5461	麗莉	Li-li	Le-li
Lily	5490-5490	萊萊	Lai-lai	Lai-lai
Lucie	2692-2457	柳施	Liu-shih	Liu-si
Lucy	6424-4824	路絲	Lu-szu	Lo-si
Luke	6424-0502	路加	Lu-chia	Lo-ka
Mark	7456-0668	馬可	Ma-k'o	Ma-kho
Martha	7456-1129	馬大	Ma-ta	Ma-tai
Mary	7456-5461-0068	馬莉亞	Ma-li-ya	Ma-li-a

Mary	3854-5461	瑪 莉	Ma-li	Ma-li
Mary	3854-7787	瑪 麗	Ma-li	Ma-le
Matthew	7456-1132	馬 太	Ma-t'ai	Ma-thai
Molly	3029-0448	毛 利	Mao-li	Mo-li
Moses	2302-6007	摩 西	Mo-hsi	Mo-se
Nancy	5571-4828	蓮 絲	Lien-szu	Lian-si
Nicolas	1441-0766-2139	尼哥拉	Ni-ko-la	Ni-ko-lah
Paul	0202-5012	保 羅	Pao-lo	Po-lo
Peggy	4310-1213	碧 姬	Pi-chi	Phek-ki
Peter	1764-1779	彼 得	Pi-te	Pi-tek
Philip	5203-0550	腓 力	Fei-li	Hui-lek
Polly	1405-5461	寶 莉	Pao-li	Po-li
Ruth	6424-1779	路 得	Lu-te	Lo-tek
Sally	5446-5461	莎 莉	So-li	So-li
Samson	0639-1327	參 孫	Ts'an-sun	Chham-sun
Sarah	2320-2139	撒 拉	Sa-la	Sat-liap
Saul	2217-5012	掃 羅	Sao-lo	So-lo
Simon	6007-7024	西 門	Hsi-men	Se-bun
Susie	4790-4828	素 絲	Su-szu	So-si
Thomas	1122-7456	多 馬	To-ma	To-ma
Timothy	2251-2302-1132	提摩太	T'i-mo-t'ai	The-mo-thai
William	1218-1670	威 廉	Wei-lien	Ui-liam

Notes
1. Chinese Christian names are discussed on pp.35-37 above.
2. Comprehensive lists of English personal names with Chinese equivalents are given by Lin Shan (1994, pp.153-200), and Evelyn Lip (1994, pp.120-141).

CHINESE ALMANACS
(T'ung shu, 通書)

We have had occasion to mention Chinese almanacs, and it will be helpful to know something more about the extraordinary and intimate role that these almanacs play in the belief and practice of many overseas Chinese.[1] Such an almanac divulges its principal message to you even before you start reading it.

Superficially it may look like any modern paperback book, with a gaudy cover, but closer scrutiny will reveal that its format goes back to Chinese bookmaking practices of the 14th century AD or earlier: the pages are doubled, "wrapped back", with the printing on the exposed surface, blank on the inner surfaces. The two loose ends of each leaf are pasted at the spine, so that the folded edge became the fore edge (in Chinese 'mouth'). The "headings" are printed vertically on the folded edge, with the characteristic "fish-tail" motif. The pages are held together with four or six stab-stitches going through the whole volume at the spine, using usually red thread to hold it together, at the upper edge formed into a loop for hanging the almanac up. One may even find, in older almanacs, the "paper twists" thrust through the spine to give the book stability. The writing is in vertical columns, from top to bottom, and beginning at the right hand side of the page. (A double page is illustrated in Figure 6.) Finally the book begins at what would be (to the westerner!) the back. Even the most recent copy of such an almanac that I have, for the year 1996-97, is made up in this format. And the message embodied in this format of course is that the tradition personified by the almanac is centuries old, of venerable antiquity.

---

[1] There are two easily accessible books in English which describe these almanacs and their function: The authoritative *T'ung Shu, the Ancient Chinese Almanac*, edited by Martin Palmer, and the attractively illustrated *Chinese Almanacs* by Richard J Smith. The latter describes and compares the almanacs produced in three areas: China proper, Hong Kong and Taiwan. We will only consider the Hong Kong type, which is the one most used in the Nanyang.

The almanacs consist of some 400 pages, but the page dimension is tall and narrow, say 250 mm x 130 mm. They have gaudy covers, and (a sign that they are reproduced from many different sources) the page lay-out throughout the book varies from section to section, and there is no continuous page numbering.

The diversity of the make-up is matched by the diversity of the contents:

"From extraordinarily diverse sources has come fortune-telling, divination, geomancy, herbal medicine, physiognomy, palmistry, charms and talismans, moral codes, dictionaries, predictions ...", etc.[2] One of the sections, "the weather and farming forecasts", reminds us of a time when the work was better known as the Farmers' Almanac.

We will look at the two sections of direct interest to us, "Telegram Numeration of Chinese Characters" and "The Hundred Family Names", which have been mentioned already.

The Chinese Commercial Code (or "Telegram Numeration of Chinese Characters")

This must be a relatively new feature of the almanacs, but all copies that I have seen do include it. It varies slightly in form. A specimen from the 1950s has the basic commercial code, and utilizes Chinese numerals. Later copies seem to employ western numerals consistently. Later copies also have additional entries to denote dates and times, or for example western numerals and the western alphabet.

The "Hundred Surnames"

It is undeniable that the occurrence of such sections in thousands of almanacs produced year after year and sold from Hong Kong to overseas Chinese is evidence that surnames (and the associated District names) continue to occupy a place in the minds of the Chinese up to the present day. They are not simply insignificant relics of the past. It has been aptly remarked that " . . . it still shapes and informs the lives of millions of Chinese today . . ." making it "a religio-cultural book of outstanding importance".[3] Furthermore,

---

[2] Palmer, 1993:9.

[3] Palmer, 1993:10.

the inclusion of the material on family names in the almanac "testifies to the enduring importance of the family and one's home area in Chinese social life". [4]

As regards layout, the arrangement of surnames is uniform in all the almanacs I have seen, that is not only regarding the order,[5] but also the arrangement in columns is the same. It seems that the District names are always included. Many also indicate the tone for the pronunciation of each character. And it is usual to carry at the top of the page small drawings of illustrious persons bearing one of the surnames on the page.

Figure 6 illustrates this. It will be seen that the names are written in groups of four, reading downwards. To the right of the small square occupied by each surname is the District name. The chief pronunciations of the first eight names, given in the right hand column (reading downwards) are:

	Wade-Giles (CCC no.)	Pinyin	Hokkien	Cantonese	Hakka	District name (Prov.) (Mathews Dict. no.)
1	Chao (6392)	Zhao	Teo	Chiu	Chhau	T'ien-shui (Shensi) (M6361 M5922)
2	Ch'ien (6929)	Qian	Chee	Chien	Chien	P'êng-ch'êng (Kiangsu) (M5060 M380)
3	Sun (1327)	Sun	Sng, Soon	Swin	Soon	Lo-an (Shantung) (M4129 M26)
4	Li (2621)	Li	Lee	Lei	Lee	Lung-hsi (Kansuh) (M4276 M2460)
5	Chou (0719)	Zhou	Chew	Chau	Choo	Ju-nan (Honan) (M3142 M4620)
6	Wu (0702)	Wu	Goh	Ng	Ng	Yen-ling (not given) (M7342 M4067)
7	Chêng (6774)	Zheng	Teh	Cheng	Chang	Yung-yang (Honan) (M7586 M7265)
8	Wang (3769)	Wang	Ong	Wong	Wong	T'ai-yüan (Shansi) (M6020 M7725)

---

[4] Smith, 1992:66.

[5] In his discussion of "The Hundred Family Names" on pp.154-6, Palmer illustrates and gives romanized forms for what at first sight may appear to be the first twenty-four names on page 1; in fact in the conventionally accepted order of the names, what he gives are nos. 1-4, 9-12, 17-20, 25-28, 33-36 and 41-44.

Notes

1. The romanized spelling of most of the District names can be found in Giles, pp.1361-63.
2. The District names for these eight names are identical with those found in Giles except for Wu (our No.6); for this surname Giles (pp.1362, 1363) gives Po-hai. (He also gives this as an alternative District name for Li (our No.4).)
3. The names of the Provinces given in the right hand column follow Giles, p.1363.
4. Some almanacs include another small character within the square of each surname, to indicate the tone of the word.
5. The figures shewn are examples of illustrious men having the surnames given below them.
6. The illustration (Figure 6) shows a wrapped back page extracted from the almanac and opened out to show in fact two adjacent pages. The printed area is 178 mm high and 200 mm wide. In the centre, in traditional style, can be seen the title 'Pai Chia Hsing' ("Hundred Family Names"), below which the fish-tail motif, and near the foot the page number ("1"). The physical make-up of the almanac is very redolent of the traditional format of Chinese books.

SOURCES

Ball, J. Dyer.
1900. *Things Chinese: being Notes on Various Subjects connected with China.* London: Sampson Low.

Bauer, Wolfgang.
1957. *Das P'ai-hang-system in der Chinesischen Personennamengebung* ZDMG 107 595-634.
1959. *Der Chinesische Personenname* [The Chinese Personal Name] (Wiesbaden:Otto Harrassowitz).

Berkowitz, M. I., F.P. Brandauer & J. H. Reed.
1969. *Folk Religion in an urban setting, a study of Hakka villagers in transition.* Hong Kong: Christian Study Centre.

Boltz. William G.
1994. *The origin and early development of the Chinese writing system.* (American Oriental Series. 78) New Haven: American Oriental Society.

Boodberg, P. A.
1938. Marginalia to the Histories of the Northern Dynasties. *Harvard Journal of Asiatic Studies* 3: 223-53.
1939. The Chronogrammatic Use of Animal Cycle Terms in Proper Names. *Harvard Journal of Asiatic Studies*: 4, 273-75.
1940. Chinese Zoographic Names as Chronograms. *Harvard Journal of Asiatic Studies*: 5, 128-36.

Bruin, A G. de.
1918.De Chineezen ter Oostkust van Sumatra. Leiden: Oostkust van Sumatra-Instituut.

Burkhardt, V.R.
1956. *Chinese Creeds & Customs*, Vol 2. Hong Kong: South China Morning Post.

Campbell, W.
1913. *A Dictionary of the Amoy Vernacular.* Tainan: Ho Tai Hong.

Chang, Hj Yusuf.

1981. Muslim Minorities in China: An Historical Note. *Journal, Institute of Muslim Minority Affairs* 3 no. 2, 30-34.

C.I.A.

1961. *Chinese Personal Names.* U.S.A.: Central Intelligence Agency.

Couvreur, S.

1916. *Cérémonial, texte chinois et traduction.* [The I Li]. Hsien Hsien: Imprimerie de la Mission Catholique. [See also Steele.]

Creamer, T.B.I.

1995. Chinese Place and Personal Names. In L. Zgusta et al (eds.) *Namenforschung*, pp.906-912. Berlin, New York: Walter de Gruyter.

Cushman, J.W. and **Wang Gungwu.**

1988. *Changing Identities of the Southeast Asian Chinese since World War II.* Hong Kong: The University Press.

Dennys, N.B.

1876. *The Folk-lore of China, and its affinities with that of the Aryan and Semitic races.* London: Trubner & Co. Hongkong: China Mail Office.

Doolittle, Justus.

1868. *Social Life of the Chinese. A Daguerreotype of Daily Life in China.* London: Sampson Low, Son, and Marston.

Doré, Henry.

1914. *Researches into Chinese Superstitions.* Shanghai: T'usewei Printing Press.

Douglas, Carstairs.

1899. *Chinese-English Dictionary of the Vernacular or spoken language of Amoy.* London: Presbyterian Church.

Feuchtwang, Stephan.

1992.*The Imperial Metaphor: Popular religion in China.* London: Routledge.

Franke, Wolfgang and **Chen Tieh Fan.**
1982,1985,1987. *Chinese Epigraphic materials in Malaysia.* Vols. 1, 2, 3. Kuala Lumpur: University of Malaya Press.

Freedman, Maurice.
1957.*Chinese Family and Marriage in Singapore.* London: H.M.S.O.

Freedman, Maurice & Marjorie Topley.
1961. 'Religion and Social Realignment among the Chinese in Singapore'. *Journal of Asian Studies* 21 3-23.

Giles, H.A.
1892. *A Chinese-English Dictionary.* London:Bernard Quaritch, and Shanghai &c: Kelly & Walsh. In a few instances reference has been made to the 1912 edition of this dictionary.

Granet, Marcel.
1930. *Chinese Civilization.* London: Kegan Paul.

Goodrich, Anne S.
1991. *Peking paper gods: a look at home worship.* Nettetal :Steyler Verlag.

Groot, J J M de.
1885. *Het Kongsiwezen van Borneo.* [Kongsi Organisation in Borneo] The Hague: Martinus Nijhoff.
1892-1910. *The Religious System of China.* 6 vols. Leyden: E J Brill.

Hauer, Erich.
1926. Das Po-kia-sing. *Mitteilungen des Seminars für Orientalische Sprachen an der Friedrich-Wilhelms-Universität zu Berlin.* 29 115-169 & 30 1927 19-85.

Hirth, F, and **W W Rockhill.**
1911. *Chau Ju-Kua: His work on the Chinese and Arab Trade in the twelfth and thirteenth centuries, entitled Chu-fan-chi.* [He wrote it about 1250 AD] [St Petersburg.] Reprinted Taipei: Ch'eng-Wen Publishing Company.

Jones, Russell.
1959. Chinese Names. JMBRAS Vol. 32 pt. 3.

Kiang Kang-hu.
1934. *On Chinese Studies*. Shanghai: The Commercial Press.

Lin Shan.
1994. *What's in a Chinese Name*. Singapore: Federal Publications.

Lin Yutang.
1947. *The Importance of Living*. London: William Heinemann.

Lip, Evelyn.
1994. *Choosing Auspicious Chinese Names*. Singapore: Times Books International.

Mathews, R H.
1952. *Chinese-English Dictionary*. Cambridge, Massachusetts: Harvard University Press.

Mau, Edward Seu Chen. 1989. *The Mau Lineage*. Honolulu: Hawaii Chinese History Center.

Newell, W.H.
1962. *Treacherous River, a study of Rural Chinese in North Malaya*. Kuala Lumpur: University of Malaya Press.

Newnham, Richard.
1971. *About Chinese*. Penguin Books.

Nio Joe Lan
1933. Iets over Chineesche namen en over het Chineesch in Indonesië. *De Indische Gids*, vol. 55, 1, 410-18.

Palmer, Martin (ed.), with **Mak Hin Chung, Kwok Man Ho** and **Angela Smith.**
1993. *T'ung Shu, the Ancient Chinese Almanac*. Kuala Lumpur: Vinpress.

Pillsbury, Barbara L.K.
1981. The Muslim Population of China: Clarifying the Questions of Size and Ethnicity. In *Journal, Institute of Muslim Minority Affairs*, 3 no. 2, p.35-58.
1983/4. Muslim Population in China according to the 1982 Census. In *Journal, Institute of Muslim Minority Affairs*, 5 no. 1, p.231-3 .

Pitcher, P.W.
1912. *In and about Amoy*. Reprinted Taipei: Ch'eng Wen Publishing 1972.

Priest, Alan R.
1955. 'Seals' in *Encyclopedia Britannica*, edn. London.

Putonghua-Minnanfangyan cidian,
1982. Fujian: Renminchubanshe. [A Mandarin and Minnan dictionary]

Rattenbury, H B.
1946.*Through Chinese eyes*. London: Edinburgh House Press.

Seidel, Anna.
1983. Imperial Treasures and Taoist Sacraments; Taoist Roots in the Apocrypha. In *Mélanges chinois et bouddhiques*, 21, 291-371.

Smith, Richard J.
1992. *Chinese Almanacs*. In *Images of Asia* Series. Hong Kong : Oxford University Press.

Sprenkel, O P N B van der.
1963. Chinese Personal Names. In C H Philips (Ed.) *Handbook of Oriental History*. London: Royal Historical Society.

Steele, John. 1917. *The I-Li, or book of Etiquette and Ceremonial*. 2 vols. London: Probsthain & Co. [See also Couvreur.]

Stepanchuk, Carol and **Charles Wong.**
1993. *Mooncakes and Hungry Ghosts: Festivals of China*. Kuala Lumpur: S. Abdul Majeed & Co.

Tan Chee-beng.
1988A. *The Baba of Melaka*. Kuala Lumpur: Pelanduk Publications.
1988B. Structure and change: Cultural Identity of the Baba of Melaka. BKI 144, p.297-314.

Tan Pow Tek.
1924.*The Pek Kah Seng*. Kuala Lumpur: Khee Meng Press.

T'ien Ju-k'ang.
1956. *The Chinese of Sarawak*. The London School of Economics and Political Science.

Watson, Rubie S.
1986. The named and the nameless: gender and person in Chinese society. *American Ethnologist* 13(4), 619-31.

Weig, P. Johann.
1931. *Die chinesischen Familiennamen nach dem Büchlein*. Tsingtau: Missionsdruckerei.

Williams, C A S.
1932. *Outlines of Chinese Symbolism and Art Motifs*. Shanghai: Kelly & Walsh.

Wojtasiewicz, Olgierd.
1954. The Origin of Chinese Clan Names, *Rocznik Orientalistyczny* 19, p.22-44.

Yen Ching-Hwang.
1981. Early Chinese Clan Organizations in Singapore and Malaya. JSEAS 12 No.1, 62-92.

Abbreviations
BKI   *Bijdragen tot de Taal-, Land- en Volkenkunde (Leiden)*.
JMBRAS   *Journal of the Malayan Branch, Royal Asiatic Society (Kuala Lumpur)*.
JSEAS   *Journal of South East Asian Studies (Singapore)*.
ZDMG   *Zeitschrift der Deutschen Morgenländischen Gesellschaft*.

Chinese Index

Mandarin Index

215

General Index

217